By Hook or by Crook

Other Books by Jill Briscoe:

Caleb's Colt
Evergrowing, Evergreen
Faith Enough to Finish
Fight for the Family
Harrow Sparrow
Here Am I—Send Aaron
How to Follow the Shepherd When You're Being Pushed Around by the Sheep
Hush, Hush
The Innkeeper's Daughter
Jonah and the Worm
Prime Rib and Apple
Queen of Hearts
Thank You for Being a Friend
There's a Snake in My Garden
Wings
Women in the Life of Jesus

With Stuart Briscoe:
Desert Songs
Mountain Songs
River Songs
Songs from Deep Waters
Songs from Green Pastures
Songs from Heaven and Earth
Songs of Light

With Judy Golz:
Space to Breathe, Room to Grow

By Hook or by Crook

How God Shaped a Fisherman Into a Shepherd

By
Jill Briscoe

WORD BOOKS
PUBLISHER
WACO, TEXAS
A DIVISION OF
WORD, INCORPORATED

BY HOOK OR BY CROOK

Library of Congress Cataloging-in-Publication Data

Briscoe, Jill.
By hook or by crook.

1. Peter, the Apostle, Saint. 2. Christian life—1960- . I. Title.
BS2515.B74 1987 225.9'24 86-32517
ISBN 0-8499-0561-3
ISBN 0-8499-3077-4 (paperback)

Printed in the United States of America

CONTENTS

To PETER, our youngest son who, like his namesake,
is being changed into a man after God's own heart,
and who carries his shepherd's staff with
humor, love, and considerable skill.

PREFACE

One way or another, Jesus insists on changing us into His image. He catches us unawares, captivates our hearts, and sets about bringing out the best in us—so we can set about bringing out the best in others. He grows a shepherd's heart in selfish people and uses them to change their world. And no one better illustrates these truths than the man called Simon whom the Lord changed "by hook or by crook" into the man called Peter.

God uses the familiar circumstances in our lives to get us into spiritual shape. In Peter's case, it happened to be things such as fish, boats, roosters, and pigs that helped transform him into a shepherd after God's heart.

I hope these pages will help you see the "Peter" possibilities in all of us.

Chapter 1

BOATS

Matthew 14:22–27

Immediately Jesus made the disciples get into the boat and go on ahead of him to the other side, while he dismissed the crowd. After he had dismissed them, he went up into the hills by himself to pray. When evening came, he was there alone, but the boat was already a considerable distance from land, buffeted by the waves because the wind was against it. During the fourth watch of the night Jesus went out to them, walking on the lake. When the disciples saw him walking on the lake, they were terrified. "It's a ghost," they said, and cried out in fear. But Jesus immediately said to them: "Take courage! It is I. Don't be afraid."

Matthew 14:22–27

Bad Weather

You can't avoid all the bad weather in life. You can try to anticipate some of it, but much is unavoidable and must be faced. On occasion there is no alternative but to sail right through the eye of the storm. Peter was about to learn this very salutory lesson.

The big fisherman was in terrible trouble. He had a battered boat, a terrified crew—and Jesus wasn't there! The Lord had just fed five thousand people, then stayed behind to send the crowds away. He told Peter and the disciples to get into the boat and set out across the Sea of Galilee. Then the storm came, and what a storm it turned out to be!

Looking back on the incident, Peter must have smiled to himself. With the advantage of hindsight he would have understood many things obscured by the terror of the moment. The boat after all was Jesus' chosen vessel to transport His disciples to their destination. Actually, it was a pretty safe place to be! Jesus came to their aid at the height of their troubles, walking on the water and thereby showing them that He truly was the God of the universe. "Tell me to come to you on the water," Peter shouted to Him above the wind. "Come," Jesus replied. So Peter did! He actually walked on the water, just like Jesus was doing. He suddenly found himself "striding over" all that he had been sinking under (Matt. 14:28–29). What an experience that must have been!

Peter would face many fierce storms before he arrived in glory, where we are told there is no bad weather to battle and all is plain sailing on a heavenly sea. Storms of doubts, despair, and ill discipline would plague him—storms of suffering and deprivation. As leader of the church, he would be caught up in hurricanes of hostility from inside the church fellowship and face headwinds from the world that would leave him just as battered and bruised as his Galilean experience. When the squalls blew up across the lake of his life, Peter must have often drawn strength from the Lord's great cry of presence and help: "Take courage! It is I. Don't be afraid."

The Church Boat

The boat in this event is a good metaphor for the church of Jesus Christ. If we try to steer the boat through the storms all by ourselves, we are in for a very rough ride indeed. And make no bones about it, it's wild out there! The wind is "contrary" or against us. Some of the disciples are resorting to survival tactics just to keep afloat, and most of us have forgotten the world of need that is waiting for us just out of sight. Talk about a boat of believers on a sea of confusion!

Yet just as surely as Jesus and the disciples were needed to minister to the multitude of troubled people waiting for them at Gennesaret (vv. 34–35), so today Jesus needs us to bring the Good News of the gospel to a hurting world. It is Christ's great desire to transport us to the point of need in His "church boat"!

There are many pictures of the church in the Bible—metaphors similar to the boat image I am using. In 1 Peter, the church is described as a building made not of bricks but of bodies (2:4–6). In Ephesians, Paul says the church is like a body with many parts, each indispensable to the whole and all subject to Christ, who is the head (4:15–16). In another passage, the church is likened to a bride, whose bridegroom is Christ (5:22–33).

Now, it's easy to knock the church, to take each of these pictures and metaphors and cynically say that the building is in need of repair, the body is sick, the bride ugly, and the boat about to sink to the bottom of the sea! But we need to remind ourselves, as my husband puts it, that "church is not somewhere you go, but something *you are.*" *We* are the church, and therefore we are accountable and responsible to God for the part we play. Perhaps ours is the brick that is chipped and doesn't quite fit, or mine is the blemished member of the body. Maybe we even sit in the boat wet and bedraggled, ready to pull in the oar because we are the ones who have stopped reckoning on the Lord Jesus Christ's stilling the storm for us. It's so easy to blame the disciple next to us for not pulling his weight, when all the time our own paddle is dragging in the water!

We need to ask ourselves a very pertinent question: Are we part of the problem or part of the solution? If Jesus has chosen us to be His disciples and has told us to get into the boat in the first place, has He called us to the task simply to frustrate us, to tease us, or because He expects us to get the job done? Surely the answer is—to get the job done!

Once we are convinced that the "church boat" is Jesus' way to transport us to a waiting world, we need to realize we are not going to have plain sailing. We must address the storm! But Jesus will help us. He does not intend for us to be at the mercy of the waves, driven backwards.

Current Currents

What then are some of the "contrary winds" and "dangerous currents" of the day that would confuse us and cause us to lose direction? First of all there is the crime wave. Domestic violence is on the increase. Hundreds are murdering members of their own families, and every single minute little children are being abused. In California, thousands of fetuses have been discovered in trash cans or dumpsters. The wave of immorality has spawned best-selling books on such subjects as how to live with herpes or ways to have sex without getting AIDS. Pornography is big business and brings in big bucks.

The church faces the same hurricane of hatred that Peter battled so long ago. To be a Christian is a costly undertaking in many parts of the world. In some places, fathers even poison their own children who decide to follow Jesus. Clouds of cults sidetrack other young believers, while the subtle reign of secularism discounts the miraculous and tries to convince us that true Christianity is irrelevant. Young people are constantly sold a bill of goods by the media concerning their sexuality. And "new theology" that sounds "chic" and "in" channels even steady churchgoers into extreme theological stances.

No wonder the apostle Paul exhorts us to grow up and "no longer be infants, tossed back and forth by the waves, and blown here and there by every wind of teaching and by the cunning and craftiness of men in their deceitful scheming" (Eph. 4:14). And it is little wonder the boat of believers is wallowing around while laboring leaders desperately try to keep the vessel on a straight course!

One of the main problems is that so much of the water is in so much of the boat! The church itself is experiencing a storm of sorrow. Hundreds of mature, thinking, caring Christians are in the depths of despair about the whole situation, with too many committing spiritual or even physical suicide. Alcohol and drugs are common ways of escape, and even the parsonage feels the effects. No wonder Christian parents are finding themselves "all at sea" as they try and raise their kids to know and love the Lord!

Women whose marriages have fallen apart and who now feel like statistics rather than persons sit in church or sing in the choir, all the while wondering if they are really accepted by the intact Christian families around them. Their children, products of those shipwrecked relationships, decide it is better to live with their boyfriends or girlfriends till they are "sure" about each other rather than make Mom and Dad's mistake. These teenagers are not way-out street kids, but rather our own churched youngsters. The water is truly in the boat. No wonder the elders of the church are bedraggled!

Smaller children go to bed to dream about a brother or a sister they can see only on weekends or to grapple with a nightmare that has them chasing elusive shadows they "think" they recognize as their own parents. Nothing in their Sunday school lesson seems to address their hurts, either. All too often the church curriculum is altogether waterlogged!

A Sunday school teacher told me about a small boy who told her he'd been "trashed." She discovered this was the way the children described themselves at school if their father or mother had left them. That same teacher was able to help that little boy to trust Jesus to be his Savior and friend. That made a huge difference in his little life, especially when he realized that the world "trashed" Jesus Christ, so He fully understood what it felt like! But more importantly, he came to believe that his heavenly Father would never "trash" him, and that gave him a marvelous sense of inner security.

That's what Christ intends for His church boats; He wants us to actually reach the "other side of the lake," where little boys who feel like they've been "trashed" need to hear about the Lord. So why are so few of us making it? All too often, unfortunately, the craven crew is going around in circles getting nowhere!

Unbelieving Believers

That brings me back to the original crew of believers on the Sea of Galilee. Think of Peter back on the churning waters of the lake, struggling to keep the boat on course. I'm sure he felt like complaining to the Lord, when he saw Him, that He might at least have allowed him to pick his own crew! Peter must have wished that all the disciples had been seasoned sailors.

But Peter had to learn that Jesus always picks His men. That's not our job; it's His. If all twelve had been fishermen, they would not have been much use once they arrived back on dry ground! And anyway, Jesus knew all about the storm before it ever hit the little boat and had made provision for it. Peter, like you and me, needed to understand that the Christ of God knows all about the weather and the people who will weather it! His cheeks wet with salt spray, Christ experienced all of the storm that His disciples experienced, yet He knew as His disciples could not know the way to walk above it all and hush the sea to sleep. It wasn't a question of picking a perfect crew, because it wasn't the crew's efforts that would win the day, but rather the intervention of the divine Jesus.

If Peter was busy wishing for a trained crew, I can't help wondering what the rest of the eleven were wishing for. But we can use our imaginations to peep around a wave and guess the various reactions of the men according to their characters.

We do know that all of them had one thing in common—

fear (Matt. 14:26). Fear had swamped their faith as surely as the waves had swamped their boat, so that their faith could make no difference! In other words, Jesus had a boat full of unbelieving believers on His hands.

Fear leads to a failure to function in the face of adversity—whatever the natural abilities God has endowed us with. In fact, fear can prevent our functioning in many circumstances—not only in adversity. As the limousine pulled up to the door on my wedding day, I froze with fear, totally unable to move. My mother had stood me on a white sheet in the living room so that the beautiful train of my dress would not get dirty! And there I stood frozen into immobility like Lot's wife. My sister spoke to me reassuringly, while my mother tried to snap me out of it with a sharp reminder of the wonderful way God had brought Stuart and me together. My father was no help at all, being almost immobile himself with prewedding nerves. There was nothing wrong with my faith. I believed without any doubt I was marrying the right man, and I knew I should be moving through that door and getting into the waiting limousine, but the sheer fear of the moment had paralyzed me.

What was I frightened about? I don't know. The unknown, perhaps, or the seriousness and immensity of the vows Stuart and I were about to take. Maybe I was experiencing a sudden terror of being stared at by all the people waiting for us at the church. Who knows? And who cares in the end what strikes us down? The important thing is what lifts us up, what gets us off the white sheet.

Fear points its finger at all the things that are bound to go wrong, but faith directs our attention toward a Father who tells us, "Jesus is there." Faith lends us words to call on the power of the Holy Spirit to release us from panic's icy grip and pry open fear's fingers from around our hearts, insisting we get on with life!

But fear hates to fail! If it cannot stop us one way, it will try another. It adapts well to different circumstances, using every opportunity to rob us of the energy we need to cope. Fear leads to fights and brawls and hostility—even among brothers!

The James and John Factor

Peter must have expected to rely heavily on his business partners, James and John. After all, they were experienced fishermen who knew the Sea of Galilee like the back of their hands. But here is where problems could have arisen.

We are not sure the boat belonged to Peter, but we may assume, knowing Peter, that whether it was his or not, he had taken charge and was busy giving orders! We can also assume that James and John, nicknamed by Jesus "the sons of thunder," resented it! The sons of Zebedee had already had a confrontation with their brother disciples as they had tried to figure out who was the greatest among them (Luke 9:46). The Scriptures lead us to believe they really thought they were the greatest, so we can presume that Peter's bossy style would have really riled them.

Time was not on their side, either. It would take a lifetime to transform the thunderclouds of their personalities into sunny days, but no one had that much time! Let's face it—a competitive, combative spirit in that particular boat on that particular day was not going to get the boat home. If you have three strong men fighting for the rudder, who knows where the boat will finish up? Poor Peter—there was enough thunder around that day without adding any of the human variety!

Isn't this our present dilemma? The "James and John factor" in our fellowships means that our church boats are filled with half-made disciples whose attitude toward leadership is one of pride rather than prudence born of true humility. We have leaders jockeying for position, building their own personal empire instead of being concerned about bringing in the kingdom. In times of crisis, it is imperative that the "best" man gives the orders. But oh, how a strong, willful spirit needs tempering with the Spirit's grace, so that all of us may "esteem other[s] better than themselves" (Phil. 2:3, KJV). James and John were probably hopping mad at Peter for getting them into the mess in the first place, resented his authoritarian style, and therefore were not about to cooperate.

Have you ever faced a "son of thunder" over an issue in the

church? Do you ever get the distinct impression he is rather glad if he gets the chance to see you out of control, flailing around, failing visibly in front of a watching crew? That doesn't help get the problem solved, does it?

Inadequate Andrew

And what about Andrew? Peter would undoubtedly have been very glad to have his brother on board. They were so different that there would have been no fear of competition between the two men. And when it came to a question of who led and who followed, Andrew would undoubtedly have been pliable—he was a "leave it to Peter" kind of person.

But Andrew was hardly a solver of problems! Shortly before, in the face of a multitude of need, Andrew had looked helplessly at five loaves and two small fish. Raising his eyes to take in the huge crowd, he had desparingly said to Jesus, "How far will they go among so many?" (John 6:9).

I think Andrew would have been experiencing a profound sense of inadequacy in the face of that terrible storm—and who could blame him? But inadequacy, though quite understandable, will not get a boat into the harbor.

Have you ever worked with an Andrew—perhaps a fine person, a finder and bringer of men and women to Jesus, but powerless in the face of a storm? Years ago, as my husband and I struggled to reach unchurched teenagers, someone came up with the great idea of simply "bearding the lion in his den." At that time, local youngsters were congregating in coffeehouses by the hundreds. "Why not go and ask the managers of those places if we could sing some Christian songs and talk to the kids?" an intrepid young Christian suggested. Then an Andrew immediately spoke up. "What are we among so many?" he whined in a small depressed voice. "There's not enough of us to go around. Anyway, our music isn't nearly good enough, and I'm sure they'll laugh at us. Some of them could even be quite dangerous, and the managers are bound to say no!"

The original Andrew would have been a much greater help to Peter if he had not allowed his own inadequacy to swamp him. Fortunately, two thousand years later we did not allow our "Andrew" to dissuade or discourage us from reaching those particular young people for Christ. During the weeks that followed, teams of excited kids tied faith to their boots and marched into many of the places we never dreamed would allow us to minister and got to work!

A "What's It Going to Cost Me?" Man

And then there was Philip. I suspect Philip's mind was not on the storm at all, but rather occupied with a list of figures that were running through his mind. He was probably trying to work out a budget, wondering if there was enough money in the kitty to buy a bigger boat!

Philip seems to me to have had a real materialistic streak in him. He was a "What's it going to cost me?" man. When Jesus had challenged the disciples to go and buy bread for five thousand people, Philip had quickly computed the money it would take and expostulated, "Eight months' wages would not buy enough bread for each one to have a bite!" (John 6:7).

There is nothing wrong with being a good steward of one's resources, but Philip had to realize that money is not the whole answer. You can't "buy off" a hungry multitude—or a storm, for that matter. Money surely helps the cause of Christ, but the danger comes when people think that all they have to do is wave a dollar bill at the wind and the wind will blow itself out! Unfortunately, there are some storms that simply whip the money right out of your hand, and your generous contribution makes no difference at all!

Money can be some of the answer some of the time, but never all of the answer all of the time. There is nothing more deflating than working hard in a church program with someone asking like a broken record, "How much is it going to cost?" Now, I know that question needs to be asked, but I wonder if it needs to be asked quite so relentlessly, as if dollars and not divinity determines what happens. We certainly need to be responsible stewards of the material resources God has given us, but sometimes we forget the Lord owns the cattle on a thousand hills and that He's quite capable of selling one at market and giving us the money.

There are some situations that must be tackled without material help because there is none available! I have seen some wonderful tributes to God's faithfulness and to man's ingenuity on the mission field—as blood, sweat, tears, and lots of joyful, willing faith have created church buildings or hospitals literally out of the caked earth.

I remember the day some converted young people and I decided to open a playschool for preschoolers in a dilapidated grain warehouse near where we lived. We had very little money—probably less than two hundred dollars among us—but we did have a great belief in a great God who, we were convinced, wanted us to go on with the project. We set out with our small offerings and spent some of our precious budget on whitewash (couldn't afford paint), soap, and scrub brushes. Some of the young people we worked with went to the lumberyard and asked for throwaway pieces of wood. They then set to work sanding down the pieces (four dollars for sandpaper). A gift of varnish finished the most handsome sets of building blocks I've ever seen.

Meanwhile, the girls discovered if you mixed flour, salt, and water together a great dough is produced that is much more pliable than expensive commercial dough (approximately six dollars for flour). Railroad ties (from dumps), ropes, cardboard boxes, and more throwaway wood—plus empty beer barrels begged from breweries—created a wonderful maze of climbing equipment. Cheap dyes mixed with certain soap powder made marvelous paint (about nine dollars)! Fingers, we discovered, were much more fun than paintbrushes, and a local store gave us packing paper for painting on.

And so we spent three months getting everything ready and began to row our boat toward the shore. At last we opened the doors to the public, and on the first day three children registered! I taught for nothing, used parents as helpers, charged very little, and after a year had over one hundred children coming to our little Christian school. Eventually the proceeds from this venture paid the salaries and expenses for a youth center and outreach for the town. Faith laughed a lot, cried a lot, but said "it can be done"—and it was so!

How much did it all cost? Under two hundred dollars! We had a Philip on our team from the beginning, but I am so glad he soon stopped calculating without Christ and began to put his many financial abilities to positive work, stretching and multiplying precious pennies.

Negative Nathanael

On the other side, however, there are the Nathanaels of this world. Nathanael would doubtless have had no problem knowing that money wouldn't solve the problem of the storm. He would have known just what to do. I'm sure the guileless old Israelite was praying hard about the situation at hand.

Jesus had first met Nathanael (also referred to as Bartholomew) shortly after the old man had finished his prayer time under a fig tree, and the Lord had approvingly called him a "true Israelite." The problem is that "true Israelites" may be good pray-ers but have grave doubts about spontaneous behavior. They are always wanting to do things after the letter of the law. They usually pour cold water on new ideas.

It would probably have irritated careful, methodical Nathanael to see Peter leap over the side of the boat into the sea. "I'm sure that's not scriptural," I can just hear him muttering to Philip. "He's bound to sink! After all, I can't think of anyone in the Old Testament who walked on water!"

I have found the church boat overcrowded with Nathanaels. They are godly, serious, lovely people who abide meticulously by the letter of the law. But if the Spirit leads anyone to do an innovative thing, they either criticize the innovator or show little sympathy when he or she sinks, saying with an air of pious satisfaction, "See, I told you so!"

Sometimes it is enough to do nothing and simply pray a storm through. But at other times we need to pray and give thanks for the Peters in our lives who impulsively "dare to be a Daniel" and who brave the wild animals of nature or their world. We must always keep trying imaginative ways to bring in the kingdom. Negativism can kill creative zeal and end up moving the boat around in "safe" circles.

Doubting Thomas—and Others of Little Faith

No, Peter could assuredly have done without Nathanael's quoting Bible verses at him and causing him to doubt. After all, that was Thomas's job; he was the one who did most of the doubting around the place. "I doubt we'll make it to shore, Peter," he was "doubtless" saying right then. He was probably planning his own funeral—or if not his, certainly Peter's!

By now, Peter himself must have had enough doubts of his own to cope with. He surely must have been wondering why God had sent the storm if He was indeed the weathermaker. I mean—just whose side was He on?

I remember an extremely hard winter in Wisconsin, where Stuart and I live. Every Saturday night—or so it seemed—the heavens opened and dumped another six to eight inches of white, fluffy snow on us all. Beautiful though it was, it became a very real problem for the church. Snowplows worked all night clearing the parking lot, but people stayed home, so offerings were down, and ministries suffered. It was easy to ask (under our breath, of course, in case God happened to be listening), "Lord, just whose side are You on?"

But then doubt always has to have an explanation for everything. And as Stephen Olford once said, "If you can explain everything that is happening in your church, your church is dead!" Faith is for the hard times, when it's all too easy to ask the question, "Lord just whose side are You on?" And faith knows the Lord's answer is always the same, even in a tornado: "YOURS!" He has proved that to us again and again.

The problem is that faith seems such a fragile answer to a howling gale! And so we have a tendency to come up with our own answers. That is probably what was happening in that boat on the Sea of Galilee. Simon the Zealot was probably thinking much more pragmatically and discussing a political solution to their dilemma with Judas Iscariot. But Judas was lost, so he wouldn't have been much help at all. Matthew in all probability was trying to take notes so that he could write a best-selling book about his adventures if they ever lived to tell the tale. And maybe James, son of Alphaeus, and Thaddaeus were wondering why Jesus had picked them in the first place, as they couldn't for the life of them think of any talents or gifts they had that seemed relevant to the challenge.

What a tragic failure of faith—to think one has nothing to offer! Whenever I'm faced with people who feel that way, I usually ask them, "Would you help me do so and so?" inviting them to do a simple task that will get them involved in some sort of spiritual service. Most times they answer, "Yes, if I can." As they help, they gain confidence. And I have a chance to work with them, get to know them, and try to help them identify some of their abilities.

For the truth is that Jesus picks us very carefully. Every single one of us in the boat is of vital significance to Him. There are no faceless followers, no giftless people in God's economy. Variety is part of His plan.

The Lord had His own wonderful reasons for putting His crew of disciples together. He was building His team and had His own perfect reasons for choosing each and every one of them. Jesus had no desire to have a boat full of Peters; no team is made up of quarterbacks!

But what do you think most of those intrepid "sailors" were doing by this time? That's right—hanging over the side, sick as dogs and wishing themselves anywhere in the world other than in that bucking boat!

There are not a few in the "boat" today who are sick and tired of the whole affair, yet scared to abandon ship and brave the storm on their own. Now, as then, it is time for us all to see Jesus walking on the water. Time to hear Him say, "Be of good cheer—don't fear—I'm here!" *That's* the only thing that will make sense out of the mess.

Vintage Peter

Typically, it was Peter who threw all caution to the wind and decided to abandon the boat so that he and the Lord could "go it alone"! This was vintage Peter—audacious, impulsive, bold. And Christ, responding as I believe He always does to spontaneous acts of faith and love, was delighted with Peter's grand audacity.

It happened during the fourth watch of the night, as Jesus went out walking on the water to the beleaguered disciples. When the men saw Him, they cried out with fear, thinking they were seeing a ghost. And who can blame them? Most of us know it was Jesus, having heard the story since our earliest days, but we need to remember they hadn't heard the story and had absolutely no idea Jesus could do such a thing.

Immediately Jesus spoke to them, assuring them it was He! "'Lord, if it's you,' Peter replied, 'tell me to come to you on the water.' 'Come,' Jesus replied. Then Peter got down out of the boat and walked on the water to Jesus" (Matt. 14:28–29).

The disciples who were left behind must have watched in awe, their eyes as big as saucers. Perhaps James and John felt it was absolutely typical of Peter to draw all the attention to himself, and maybe Thomas doubted Peter would ever keep afloat. But surely all must have marveled at the supernatural power of Jesus that sustained a mere man in the face of angry nature. While Peter trusted Jesus, only his feet got wet. But when wind and wave distracted his attention, he sank beneath the waves immediately. "Lord, save me!" he cried out, and Jesus did, as He always will, chiding him for his "little faith" (v. 31).

What a vivid portrayal of the church! So many of us clutch our oars or each other, helpless in the face of the gale, yet carefully evaluating any "Peter person" who is different from ourselves. Anyone who dares to dare, who dreams his dreams into reality, who makes his visions happen, is bound to be in trouble with the rest of us. Knowing a little psychology these days, we think we've plumbed the depths of a Peter personality. And so we psychoanalyze his unconventional behavior and draw the conclusion that he has a need to be noticed. We may even decide he is acting out childhood fears or phobias.

Why can't we let people be themselves any more? Saved by grace, healed of sin and selfishness, many Christians are ready to let Jesus use their variegated characters to get the job done. Peter was being Peter, and Jesus loved him for it. He certainly rebuked him when he sank! But if He chided Peter for a lack of faith, I wonder what He had to say to the rest of the craven crew who stayed safely in the boat? I venture a guess it was so "hot" it would have burned through our Bibles clear to Revelation, so Matthew omitted it!

Reckoning with Christ

After Jesus helped Peter climb back into the boat (for remember, the boat *was* Jesus' vessel to accomplish His purposes) and the storm ceased, all the disciples came and worshiped the Lord (v. 33). They humbly acknowledged His person, His power, and His presence. And that is exactly what it is going to take to get the boat to its destination. It is realizing Jesus is God and therefore God of the storms that forces us to believe He does indeed know what He is doing—to believe no wind blows harder than it must, no rain falls longer than He wills, and no waves can capsize us when He is on board. That doesn't mean we won't get battered, bruised, and wet! But it does mean we will end up glad to be in the boat with Jesus rather than on the land without Him.

It's realizing that Jesus has power we do not have that will bring us to worship at His feet, even while the shock of our experience is hardly over. And it's acknowledging His presence that will bring such an awareness of His close companionship in our troubles and trials. Then our sails will be filled with the wind of His Spirit and drive us where He wants us to go.

The disciples needed to know there was no way they could cope with the storm without Him. I am reminded of an oft-repeated couplet from Major Ian Thomas:

> "I can't!" *"I never said you could;*
> *I will—I always said I would."*

When Jesus presented Himself in their midst, the men in the boat realized that only God could do what He had done. Surely Jesus was the Son of God!

If you and I can realize He is present with us when we are about to sink in deep waters, if we can remind ourselves:

> We can't! But then He never said we could;
> however,
> He will—He always said He would,
> then we will not be afraid!

What storm are you facing—an angry, unresponsive husband, or a child you suspect is into drugs? What current currents whirl you away from your moorings into the depths of despair—a financial disaster, a dreaded report from the hospital, a church fight among your closest friends? When you start to reckon with Jesus instead of reckoning without Him, you will find, as Peter found, that the boat will reach the shore (John 6:21). In other words, your goals will be achieved, the plan of God will be put into operation, people will be blessed. And you will do more than survive; you will be a far deeper Christian than you ever were before!

Walking on Water

"If only," I hear some of you say, "I could just see Him with my own eyes, like Peter did; that would make all the difference."

Would it? Peter saw Him clearly, and yet he sank! It's a matter of dependence. We all have the Scriptures, where Christ is clearly seen. If we will continually look in faith to Him, not at the wind and the waves of our circumstances, then we will find a tranquility within, whatever is happening without!

A friend of ours lives and works in Northern Ireland. His offices are in downtown Belfast. Some years ago, in the middle of the "troubles," as the bombings by Protestant and

Catholic extremists are called, Stuart and I went to Belfast at our friend's invitation to hold a series of meetings. While we were there, the IRA planted bombs in our friend's business complex and blew it up.

Alerted to the catastrophe by the police, we raced to the scene. It was turmoil! Dense smoke was everywhere, fire alarms kept up an insistent message, other tenants from the building dashed in and out of the charred rooms trying to salvage anything they could find from the wreckage.

We looked at our friend. He stood in the midst of this personal storm, his business in ruins all around him, and was obviously at peace. Despite his great personal loss, it was evident he was saying to himself, "The Lord gave, and the Lord hath taken away; blessed be the name of the Lord" (Job 1:21). Jesus Himself in all His power was present in this man's life, dressing his spirit in tranquility. For him the storm was without—not within. He was not afraid.

What was more, our friend clearly wanted others to know what he was experiencing! One of the firemen came by—a man whom he knew well. Our friend stopped the fireman and thanked him for doing his very dangerous job so conscientiously. Then he said, "Don't stay too late. Take your men home. Tomorrow is the Lord's day, and we all need to be ready to worship Him!"

We were all stunned—and humbled—and grateful to God for His great ability to help a man in such distress. But then we were simply witnessing a normal Christian living the extraordinary life of a believing believer—a man reaching for Christ and drawing on His power to walk on water with his Lord!

I'm sure Peter did not forget the lessons he learned on the blue Sea of Galilee. God used ordinary and familiar things like a boat, a storm, and a lake as the backdrop for a display of His divinity that took Peter's breath away! As we trace the big fisherman's steps as he followed the Master, we will see the footprints of his faith grow bolder with time, and we will probably discover that each one of us in measure is a "Peter person"!

Peter had learned that you can't avoid all the bad weather in life. Some of the storms of life you can anticipate and sail around. But often you have no alternative other than to grit your teeth and sail right through the eye of the storm! Peter was to find, to his surprise, that he would come out into the sunshine on the other side! And even in the midst of the storm—with Jesus' help, he could even walk on water!

WORKSHEET

Chapter 1

I. Read the following passages which give us a picture of the church. Say which you like and why.

   BUILDING—1 Peter 2:4–6
   BODY—Ephesians 4:16
   BRIDE—Ephesians 5:22–23
   BOAT—Matthew 14:22–23

II. What are some of the current currents or strong storms that are battering the church in your area?
   a. Make a list of them.
   b. Rank them in order of severity.

III. Make a list of the twelve disciples. (See Matt. 10:2–4; Mark 4:14–19; Luke 6:12–16; John 1:44–50. Note that some disciples are called by two names; for example, Thaddaeus is also called Judas son of James, and Nathanael is thought to be the same as Bartholomew.)
   a. Review the main characteristics of each disciple.
   b. Can you identify with any of these men? If so, which one and why?

IV. PRAYERTIME: How are we to overcome the storm? We will need to rely on Jesus' power and peace. Thank Him for the promise and reality of that.

Chapter 2

FISH

Mark 1:16–18

As Jesus walked beside the Sea of Galilee, he saw Simon and his brother Andrew casting a net into the lake, for they were fishermen. "Come, follow me," Jesus said, "And I will make you fishers of men." At once they left their nets and followed him.

Mark 1:16–18

A Big Fish

Simon caught fish for a living, so it was fitting he was about to be "caught" himself. And make no bones about it, Simon was a big fish! Oh, none of his friends thought so at the time; after all, Simon was Simon. He had a big personality, was impulsive, and was an incredibly strong, rugged character. "Take-charge Simon," he was probably called. I'm sure he was too much for many people. But then, that was before Jesus got hold of him and began a work in his heart that changed the direction of his life and fashioned his character anew. That was before Simon became Peter!

Simon worked with his brother, Andrew. They fished the lake with their business partners, old Zebedee and his two sons, James and John. They plied their trade on the shores of gorgeous Galilee, a body of water that, though beautiful, could often be turbulent and dangerous for their small fishing craft.

In telling how Peter came to follow Jesus, Mark's Gospel simply states that one day Jesus came walking along the shores of the lake, saw Peter and Andrew washing their nets, and called out to them, "Come, follow me, and I will make you fishers of men." So, the Bible says simply, "At once they left their nets and followed him" (Mark 1:17–18).

"Just like that?" you say, "they left *everything* and followed a stranger?" Well, not quite just like that! In the first place, Peter was probably *already* a disciple of Jesus when the Lord made His dramatic call to follow Him into active ministry. The Gospel of John describes how Peter *first* came to know the Lord through the influence of his brother, Andrew, and the testimony of John the Baptist (John 1:40–42).

But even then, Peter's decision to follow Jesus did not come totally out of the blue. I don't believe any conversion does! Whenever someone comes to Christ from an apparently non-Christian environment, I always find myself wondering what has been going on behind the scenes. What praying grandmother or bright Christian aunt or believing boss has been busy praying in the shadows? How many seeds of gospel truth have been planted in their hearts by friends? Invariably I find that God has been quietly at work, using the familiar things of this world—people, perhaps, or a religious upbringing, or even events in early childhood that eventually bring these folks to faith.

Waiting for the Messiah

In Peter's case, we are not told much about his religious beliefs at the time he met Jesus. But we do know about his heritage. He was a Jew, one who "waited for the consolation of Israel." What does that mean? It means he was looking for the Messiah. What did that mean to Peter?

The word *Messiah* literally means "one who is smeared with oil" or "anointed." Most frequently the word was used in the Old Testament to refer to the kings of Israel; for example, David once refused to kill a sleeping King Saul because, as he said, "The Lord forbid that I should lay a hand on the Lord's anointed" (1 Sam. 26:11). An anointed king of Israel had been set apart, chosen by Jehovah Himself to rule Israel under God and bring prosperity and blessing to bear upon His people.

David, of course, went on to become Israel's anointed king after Saul, and he was considered to be the ideal king of Israel. His rule had a sacred character in the nation's thinking. The problem was that David died and was followed by a line of lesser kings. Expectation for another like him began to fade, so the hope of Israel began to be projected into the future. The Jewish people began looking for a Messiah—an anointed king of David's lineage—who was to come "at the end of the age."

The prophets encouraged such hope for a future anointed ruler. Jeremiah talked of David's line continuing (Jer. 33). Isaiah described the Messiah's regal splendor (Isa. 9:11), and Micah talked about His birth at Bethlehem (Mic. 5:2).

However, the prophets also spoke of a Promised One who was much more than just a chosen king like David. Daniel, for example, described an incredible vision God had given him, in which he looked through the door of heaven. There he saw a God-man—a being who looked like a human and yet resembled the Almighty, and who was given a throne and a kingdom.

Isaiah, on the other hand, drew a graphic picture of another figure of great importance—the "suffering Servant." This would be a man "obedient unto death," a sacrificial Lamb who would die voluntarily to redeem men's souls.

All these elements were part of the Jewish heritage Peter brought with him when he first met the Lord. And Jesus, of course, fused all three elements together—the anointed or chosen One, the suffering Servant, and the God-man (or, as Jesus called Himself, the Son of Man). In fact, we cannot count ourselves Christian if we do not believe that Jesus Christ was indeed all three figures in one.

But this was not all clear to Peter and the rest of the disciples at the beginning. They were products of their own religious background, looking for the Messiah, but by then the concept of Messiah had become confused in people's thinking.

No wonder the disciples didn't "get it" at first when they were called to follow Jesus. The idea of an earthly king like David of old who would get rid of the Romans for them was uppermost in their minds, and the idea of a prophet was easily understood—but they were not really expecting this One who came to be an anointed King, a God-man, and a suffering Servant all in one!

Ready for the Truth

Peter's Jewish background—with the fervent, if not always accurate, expectations for the Messiah—was part of him long before he met Jesus. Add to that the influence of John the Baptist and you see that much of the truth had been sown in his fertile mind before Jesus ever came along and called him from his nets to catch men.

It was John the Baptist who first alerted everyone to the fact that Jesus was indeed Isaiah's suffering Servant who had come to save the world, and it was John who also preached so powerfully and persuasively that Jesus was the coming King. Hundreds believed, repented, and were baptized, preparing themselves to receive God's Messiah.

Andrew, Simon's brother, was one of John's disciples, so you can be sure he had been sharing the Baptist's wisdom with his brother. One day Jesus walked by, and John identified Him as the One they had been waiting for. Convinced of Jesus' identity, Andrew ran to share the greatest discovery of his life with his brother, telling him excitedly, "We have found the Messiah!" (John 1:41).

So all this was preparation for the day Peter made his dramatic decision to leave everything and go with Jesus. Peter had his Jewish tradition of hope, the testimony of John, the influence of Andrew, and probably several months of observing the Master firsthand.

What influences can you count in your past that have pointed you to the Christ of God? Was it a solid church background or some religious relative whom you couldn't quite understand but who helped you see glimmers of spiritual truth? Or perhaps it was a book passed on to you by a neighbor. Maybe a television show caught your attention, or a friend's changed life sparked your interest. Perhaps it was none of these things, but rather the still, small voice of conscience that told you you needed a Savior.

For me it was a sunrise. At least, that is where it all began. I was vacationing with my parents in Switzerland at the age of fourteen. We could find no accommodations for the night, so we decided to sleep in the car. It was a small vehicle, and no one could really get any rest. Giving up, I got out of the car and wandered to a small ridge overlooking the fabulous Swiss Alps. And there I watched the sunrise.

It's the Book of Romans that tells us God has revealed Himself in nature, but I had never read the Book of Romans, or any other Scripture for that matter. I did, however, "read" that sunrise and a huge sense of God's glory overwhelmed me. Along with that came a corresponding consciousness of my own unworthiness.

Going back to the car, I penned a poem of sorts:

The day breaks softly, filling me with awe.
It seems the other side of heaven's door.
That God forgives my sins, to me is plain. . . .
Today, "spite of my sin—the sun doth rise again!"

There were other glimpses of truth in those early years. The witness of a friend, a scary spell in the hospital, and a small booklet called *Becoming a Christian* alerted me to my need. Each of us will have a different tale to tell, because we are all so different. As I discovered, there is only one road to God—"through" Jesus—but there are *many* roads to Jesus.

A New Name

Simon, responding to the various ways the Spirit of God had worked in his life, willingly accepted his brother's invitation to meet Christ. Jesus met him with the words, "You are Simon son of John. You will be called . . . Peter" (John 1:42). And immediately things began to change for Peter.

Conversion, you see, has to do with change—change in name and changes in our thinking. Character change, shown in our behavior, is inevitable, and changes in our relationships are unavoidable. As 2 Corinthians 5:17 puts it, "Therefore, if anyone is in Christ, he is a new creation; the old has gone, the new has come."

It was a whole new day when Simon met the One who would make him into a Peter. Of course, it didn't happen overnight—it never does! But it's encouraging to me to know that when we meet Jesus He gives us a new name to match our new nature—a new name with the promise of new potential—just as He gave a new name to Peter. We don't know what that name is, but we can know it speaks of the person He will cause us to become through a growing relationship with Him. It will be a "character" name.

The new name Jesus gave to Simon implied a claim of authority. It was almost like the change of a name in marriage. It spoke of a new relationship, a new position. It meant Simon didn't belong to Simon anymore; he belonged to someone else.

When I got married, it was a sheer delight to take my husband's name! "Imagine his giving me his very own name to wear," I thought. "That's so special!" I delighted to hear myself introduced as Mrs. Briscoe. Not that I was ashamed of my old name, but the privilege and joy of the new was a fresh daily reminder of my new status and relationship.

Above all, my new name reminded me of my husband's love and commitment. A man's name (especially if he is an Englishman) is very important to him. It is far more than just a mailing label; it's his reputation, his character—it's him. It meant a lot for my husband to give me his name. And how proud I was as a young wife to bear it!

Yes, taking my husband's name meant a total change in every area of my life. What's more, that change took place in an instant. In a few short moments, the minister led us in our vows and then presented us to the congregation as Mr. and Mrs. Stuart Briscoe! The giving of the name took a moment. The wearing of it is taking a lifetime. But the change in my life began immediately!

In the same way, by giving Simon a new name, Christ signified an immediate consecration of character. It would be a few months before Jesus would call Peter and Andrew away from their nets. But the change in Peter was to begin immediately—with no time lapse. Simon accepted the Lord's call and *immediately* began a life of discipleship.

So many times I meet Christians who accept Christ's claims but experience a time lapse before changes take place in their lives. Perhaps they have not been instructed properly, or they may have walked forward at a meeting for the wrong motivation, or maybe they just wanted the benefits of Christianity without any responsibilities attached to it. If they were honest, they would have to admit to saying:

Wait a while, Lord.
Give me a new name later in life,
  when I'm old and have had my fun,
  when I'm ugly and can't enjoy flirting anymore,
  when I'm sick and need You to help me die—
Change me then . . .

Yes, wait a while
before You change my character;
I rather like it the way it is.
There're some grubby little things in my life
that won't take kindly to change . . .

What's that?!
You love me too much to let me be a "time-lapse" Christian?
There's a close encounter of the most intimate kind
involved in being the Christian
You've called me to be?
Oh no! It's up to *me* to follow and cooperate—
to trust and obey You now?

Well! I didn't bargain for this;
I didn't understand all that when I came to Christ . . .
You understand it now, My child.
Leave your nets and follow me.

A Change in Character

Being a Christian means a change of character brought about by discipleship, beginning the moment you meet Jesus. By change of character I don't mean a change of *personality,* but rather the ability to handle your personality, to enhance it and find its full potential. For example, the person who is lazy by nature will probably be a pretty laid-back character, fun to be with. After accepting Christ, this sort of person should be even more fun to be with, and Christ will help him not to allow his strengths to be his weaknesses anymore.

Our daughter is an extremely conscientious girl. She is an overachiever who doesn't particularly enjoy overachieving! So many times while growing up she would say with great intensity such things as, "Why can't I be like my brothers and take life a little easier? Why do I *always* have to get an A when a B would be perfectly acceptable? I wish I could be like them!"

One day a wise friend told her, "Judy, you'll always be Judy. God made you with this type of personality. But He will help you to 'handle' yourself, to cope with your strengths, which are also your weaknesses." That piece of advice was an enormous help to our daughter.

How often do Simons wish they were Andrews, Philips wish they were Nathanaels, Matthews wish they were Peters! That is an exercise in futility. Christ changes for the better what is best and helps us cope with the things that are lacking in our personalities. He does this in many ways, one of the most common being to link us up with others who can balance out the deficiencies.

One way or another, Christ will enable us to accept our inability to be what He never created us to be! But make no bones about it, Christ always perfects our potential over time and eternity. That is, Christ always finishes what He begins. I've never seen an unfinished sunset or a perfect bird with one wing—have you? We can be confident of this: "that he who began a good work in you will carry it on to completion until the day of Christ Jesus" (Phil. 1:6).

During the early years of our marriage, my husband and I worked with young people in Europe as part of a missionary organization. When that assignment was over and we had to move to America and leave those lovable teenagers we had been working with, I found myself struggling emotionally. We had seen many of these young people come to Christ from really raw backgrounds. They had kicked the drug habit, cleaned up their sex lives, and begun to show radical changes in their behavior. What would happen if their leaders just "disappeared," I worried. Would they go on with God?

My husband reminded me, "You didn't save them; you don't have to keep them, Jill!" No, the work in them was not finished. They were "in the making" and in no wise "made"—but the God who had begun that changing work in their hearts had promised to complete it, and I could safely leave them in His hands.

A "Because-You-Say-So" Life

Of course, the individual has a responsibility in this process too. We need to cooperate by being obedient, which is a key to discipleship. If we will only choose to live a "because-You-say-so life," we will find a change happening inside and outside. Oh, the Lord may command us to follow Him as a preacher or tell us to follow Him as a fisherman, but either way obedience will change us, and the change will most certainly be for the better!

Look at the story in Luke 5, which tells in more detail the story Mark gives so briefly. Peter was still fishing, even though he had taken time off to help the young preacher from Nazareth. On this particular occasion, the disciples had toiled all night and caught nothing. But the Lord told them, "Put out into deep water, and let down the nets for a catch" (v. 4).

Peter, obviously feeling Jesus should stick to preaching and leave him to figure out his trade, reluctantly complied. "Because you say so, I will let down the nets," he muttered (v. 5). Peter probably respected the Lord too much to tell Him that fish generally feed in the dark and not in the light, and seeing they had toiled all night and caught nothing it was highly improbable that they would come up with anything in broad daylight. When they had done as Jesus said, however, "they caught such a large number of fish that their nets began to break" (v. 6)!

How like us this is! We think Jesus needs to live in the religious section of our lives. He can look after that part, we say, but He can't really understand the secular part of us. "What can He know about my job?" we question. "After all, I have a masters degree!"—or the technical school diploma or the training certificate. So, we reason, we'll look after that bit.

We need to grow to understand that if we are fishermen, He, the Maker of fish and men, is the expert and can make us far better fishermen than others ever could. If we are teachers, He, the greatest of all teachers, can make us better educators than we could ever be through our own self-effort. If we are mathematicians, He, who brought to birth the laws of the universe, can lend us His help!

Peter, overwhelmed with the miracle of the fishes, finally began to grasp this fact. Here was no mere religious guru, but more—perhaps even God? No wonder Peter responded to the amazing miracle with the words, "Go away from me, Lord; I am a sinful man" (Luke 5:8). (A sense of insufficiency was not, I guess, a common experience for Peter. From "I am a sufficient man" to "I am a sinful man" is a long step in the right direction.) And it was after this that Peter left everything to follow Jesus.

Opening the doors of the things we do best opens the world to us! It is no accident, in my mind, that Daniel and his God-fearing friends were described as ten times better than all the other bright young men in the university (Dan. 1:20). When you know God, you have to have an edge over those who don't know Him. Haven't you found, as I most definitely have, that coming to know Christ sharpens your focus and enhances all aspects and disciplines of your life?

Peter came to realize that Jesus could teach him something about fishing, not just something about preaching. We must realize that, too. So often we keep Christ for Sundays and let "Peter" loose for the rest of the week!

Once I faced a situation similar to Peter's. I had a new teaching post in Liverpool and set about my work with great enthusiasm. I knew I could teach, had lots of creative ideas, and was highly thought of by my staff. On the weekends, I helped to run a church youth program that gave me lots and lots of opportunities to trust the Lord!

I thought I had myself in the correct perspective. On Saturdays and Sundays, I prayed hard, trusted God, made sure I was in my Bible, and felt my very small piece of the action was pretty insignificant. But Monday to Friday was an altogether different matter! In other words, I reckoned Jesus could rely on me on weekdays; I would rely on Him on weekends!

Then it dawned on me that Jesus wanted to be fully involved in my classroom! I discovered He actually knew more about second- and third-graders than I did. So I began to "trust and obey" at school as well as at church, and I was amazed at the results. Before, I had managed to do my "fishing"—or rather my teaching—with an average amount of success. Now nets began to break; so many wonderful things were happening I needed help from others just to keep up! When I learned to allow Him to direct my every activity, the difference was astonishing.

Going Deeper—and Leaving Our Nets

It's hard to learn dependence when you've done a halfway decent job without it. But as we come to know the Lord in reality, we deepen as people in every dimension. And it is then we realize just how much we need His help.

Remember, Jesus challenged Peter to "put out into the deep water" (Luke 5:4). Stop hugging the shore, Peter—launch out, go deeper—He had said. And that is exactly what He says to us. "Going deeper" for us may not involve oars, water, and fish. Perhaps it will involve digging deeper into our Bibles and learning new skills that will help us discover the truths of obedience and faith.

Going deeper may even mean developing abilities we never knew we had. "Don't be afraid; from now on you will catch men," Jesus promised Peter (Luke 5:10). Now that was scary; Peter may have been skilled at catching fish, but he had little idea how to go about catching people! Still, Jesus told Peter not to be afraid. "You *will* catch men," the Lord said. He didn't say, "Would you like to catch men?" or "You might, if you're lucky, catch a man." He promised Simon Peter that he *would* be a fisher of men.

And of course, the Lord says the same thing to us. Jesus has said that all His disciples are to be "fishers of men"—wherever we work and whatever we do. Not every person will be a gifted preacher, but the Bible does say we all must be involved in the business of winning others to Christ.

How can we learn to do this? First, we will need to abandon our nets, just as those early disciples "left everything" and followed Him.

Now, God may never call us, as He called Peter and the others, to leave our occupations and become involved in some sort of full-time ministry employment. Then again, He may; we all need to be at least open to the possibility, to try to pray genuinely, "Lord, I am willing to go" without secretly planning to stay. But whether or not we change our actual occupations, we *must* cultivate a mental attitude of abandonment to Him.

Nets can be a symbol of many different things—not just employment. Maybe our minds get entangled with materialism or our hearts get caught up in a relationship that chokes the life right out of us. God's Spirit can free us from such entanglements and give us a great desire to pick up a rod and go fishing. Nets can be bad habits or good habits. Anything that stops our being obedient can end up preventing us from becoming a fisher of men! So an ongoing attitude of abandonment to Jesus must become operative in our lives.

Remember that our personality will not change when this happens, although our behavior must. And often the same skills that have been easy for us to master can simply be transferred to spiritual things.

For example, Peter's best attributes were his skills as a fisherman. They involved watchfulness and patience. He needed courage to take his life in his hands on fickle Galilee day by day. Peter needed to transfer all these natural abilities and trained skills to his new calling. He would need all his gifts in the work that Jesus gave him to do.

Before I knew Christ, I enjoyed art. When I was converted, I simply directed that skill in a spiritual direction. I found I was able to write Christian plays and use my artistic training to paint backdrops or design sets. Before I knew the Lord, I played tennis for my school. Once I knew Jesus, even this skill found a place in the youth ministry. I was able to organize a youth tennis tournament that ended with a pig roast and a concert by a Christian music band; then a short gospel presentation was made and "fish" were caught! Jesus not only made me a better teacher, but He also used these teaching skills long after I had left the classroom to serve Him in ministry.

Keeping Our Distance

Following Jesus is a lifelong business. Peter started off very well; he met Jesus and his life immediately began to change—

remember there are no "time lapse" Christians! When Jesus asked, Peter left his nets and followed the Master.

But there came a time when Peter put a bit of distance between himself and his Lord. In fact, the Scriptures tell us of a time when Peter "followed [Jesus] at a distance" (Matt. 26:58). Now, that means trouble. Once we start doing that, it is hard to hear the Lord's voice, and that means we can't continue to be obedient!

After three years of faithful following, of being with Jesus when He made the blind to see, the lame to walk, and the deaf to hear, Peter found himself faced with the challenge of his life. At first it had been fun to help the *popular* preacher. But as time passed, the crowds that had been so appreciative began to be intimidated by those who hated Jesus and wanted Him destroyed. Things changed. Now it was the *problem* preacher that Peter found himself defending.

When Judas led the priests and soldiers to Gethsemane, Peter attacked one of the men and was soundly rebuked for it by Jesus, whom he was only trying to protect! It was all too much for Peter, and he took to his heels and ran. But Peter didn't run far. He kept the mob in sight and, in fact, did a very brave thing. He began to follow "at a distance" to see what would happen.

But that's where the trouble began! Following "afar off," as the King James Version puts it—or putting distance between Jesus and ourselves by refusing to fully identify with Him in His suffering—leads to terrible trouble. Peter was undoubtedly brave, but he wasn't brave enough!

The result of following "afar off" was traumatic for Peter. He ended up denying the Lord with oaths and curses. It was then he did something we all tend to do when we slip and fall—he tried to get away from the "scene of his crime." He went back home to his boats and fish—and, incidentally, to his nets!

It was there that the risen Christ found Peter and called him once more as he fished his beloved Galilee. Jesus appeared on the lakeshore and called out to the men in the boat, "Haven't you any fish?" (Luke 21:5). Peter and the other men who were with him, replied, "No." "Throw your net on the right side of the boat and you will find some," Jesus said. So they did, and immediately they caught a huge amount of fish—one hundred fifty-three in all. That was enough to trigger an obvious response from the disciples: "It is the Lord!" John shouted. At that, Peter jumped over the side of the boat to swim to shore. "There he goes again!" James surely said to John. But Jesus, used to Peter's spontaneous and dramatic reactions, simply said, "Come and have breakfast."

Breakfast with Jesus

In my own experience, I have been invited to many such breakfasts with Jesus. These have been times to say I'm sorry for denying Him and times to hear Him tell me I'm forgiven and send me on my way.

I learned early in my Christian experience to try and keep short accounts with God—not to let a huge pile of things stack up between us before we have that vital breakfast meeting. But I have also discovered that if I return to my entanglements He will not leave me there. He will first require honesty from me. He will ask me if I have caught any fish lately, and I will need to answer truthfully, "No!" Then, if indeed my life has been barren and unfruitful, He will show me how to redress the situation. When I cease to be effective, it's time to have breakfast with Jesus.

Remember, Peter was a veteran follower of the Lord at the point in his life when he began to follow "afar off." In the early days, when the exhilaration of being with Jesus was high, Peter had begun to handle his own rod and line. Hadn't the Lord sent the disciples out two by two to preach and teach and heal? Hadn't Peter experienced power and abilities he didn't dream were possible? Oh yes. But that seemed a long, long time ago; in fact, it must almost have felt like a dream. Now, fishing for fish again Peter was experiencing failure! Why, he couldn't even succeed at his trade anymore!

There was a time in my own experience that I followed "afar off." I thought the other disciples around me were unaware of my spiritual malaise, but I knew very well the coldness and despair of my heart. I still went through the motions—teaching school, fulfilling my role at church—but I didn't have any fish on the end of my line. Even my teaching, which I loved, lost its appeal. It was the still, small voice of the Spirit that alerted me to the problem: "Have you any fish, Jill?" I seemed to hear Him say. "No Lord," I had to answer softly, "I haven't, and You know it, I know it, my brothers and sisters know it, and I expect the whole world knows it by now!" It was time to have breakfast with Jesus!

Finding the Fish

How long has it been since you had a fish on your line? Can you look back to effective days in the past when everything was different? What happened? When did you begin to follow "afar off"? And what have been the repercussions of the gap that has widened between you and the Lord? Is it time to have breakfast with Jesus?

After all, He knows what the fisherman himself needs in the way of forgiveness and restoration. And He also knows where the fish are! Once, when taxes were due, Jesus told Peter to walk down to the shore of Galilee and catch a fish in whose mouth would be a coin—enough to pay both Peter's and Jesus' taxes! Peter did exactly what Jesus told him to do, and sure enough the money was found in the fish's mouth (Matt. 17:27). Peter *knew* Jesus knew where the fish were!

So in our efforts to reach men for Christ, or to "fish for men," as Jesus put it, we need to ask Him to renew our relationship with Him and then to direct our activities. "Throw your net on the right side of the boat and you will find some," Jesus said to the men in the boat. Sure enough, that's where the fish were (John 21:6).

Once, when Stuart and I were trying to find a way to "catch" a batch of kids for Christ, we tried all sorts of standard ideas—youth meetings, special music events, camp programs. They reached a very few fish. Then someone decided to ask Jesus to show us where to cast the "net."

We spent time in prayer asking that very question, and two things soon became obvious to us all. With our "ordinary" methods of evangelism, we were quite frankly spending lots of time and energy fishing in a swimming pool! In other words, the fish we were dealing with were mostly already caught. The ones who needed catching were swimming around in the open seas—or in the multitude of muddy streams and rivers that lay well outside the placid pools of church. The Lord helped us to begin to cast our nets on the "right" side of the ship, and then we saw a great harvest. It's amazing the difference it makes when we ask Jesus where the fish are instead of deciding where they ought to be!

After accepting the call to our current church, Stuart and I set to work ministering to the people. There was already a good women's ministry going on, so I joined in enthusiastically. After a few years, hundreds of women were coming to Bible studies. Then one day a young woman asked me what I was doing about our "diminishing audience." I looked over her shoulder at the hundreds of ladies chatting to each other and wondered what on earth she meant. She told me, in effect, "You've got to cast the net on the right side of the boat."

"These fish are caught," the woman said. "There are thousands outside church boundaries." "Where are they?" I asked, taken aback. "They are in the workplace," she replied. "What's more, the women here are going back to work, too. In five years you'll have less than half of them." She was right. I needed to have breakfast with Jesus! I did, and after another exciting period of training and evangelism I saw a ministry to working women that effectively infiltrated the unplumbed depths of need in our city.

Jesus knew where the fish were—and He knows where they are today. He'll tell us—if we'll only take time out to ask Him!

Catching the Fish

Not only will Jesus help us find the fish; He will help us catch them, too. And we need His help, because fishing—real fishing—is hard work. It took many strong men working together to haul in those one hundred fifty-three fish. But Jesus promised He would make us fishers of men, and that presupposes we do our share of the finding and our share of the catching.

My father was a fisherman. I never ever heard him return from a day's fishing and announce, "I influenced a lot of fish today!" He either said, "I caught one" or "I lost one!" But how many of us stop short of actually catching our "fish"? Perhaps the work involved is just too hard for us. Maybe we are scared of actually talking to someone about receiving Jesus—in case they laugh at us or reject us.

"Jesus is living inside us, and it is His job to win souls," I was told almost as soon as I had come to Christ. I remember saying to the girl who led me to Him, "Oh, I could never share my faith with anyone else." "Yes, you can," she replied cheerfully. You don't become an expert fishermen overnight—but there have been many big fish caught by little boys with a pole and a bent pin. The important thing is enthusiasm! Our job is to be so thoroughly enamored with our Savior that we "launch out" into the deep things of the Christian faith, let our nets down in the place He tells us to, and then rely on Him as we do the hard work of hauling in the consequences of such a Christ-directed operation.

"But how *do* you actually catch a fish?" you may ask. You wait for the chance to tell people, as simply as you can, four basic facts:

1. Jesus loves them and died for them so that they can be forgiven and go to heaven (John 3:16).
2. Jesus, by His Spirit, will come and dwell in their hearts if they invite Him to (Rev. 3:20).
3. If they do invite Him in, He will come in as He promised and will forgive and empower them to be obedient.
4. Jesus will instruct them through His Word and through prayer how to change things in their lives that need changing. He will direct them into serving others in His church, and He will begin to make them fishers of men themselves!

If the people you speak to are willing to receive Christ and believe the basic facts of the Christian gospel—that God is holy, that we are sinful, and that Christ is God and died to reconcile us to Himself—then you need to ask them to pray a simple prayer with you. At this point you need to "land" the fish and not let them swim away! The words of this prayer can be very simple and yet profound—could be something like this: "Jesus, I need You. Jesus, I want You. Please by Your Spirit come to live in me. Forgive all my sin, assure me of heaven, and make me a fisher of men. Amen."

Isn't this where most of us throw in the rod? Perhaps we actually have a fish on the line. A friend at work asks us a question that gives us a chance to explain the Christian message. On the way home from Sunday school, our little girl asks us, "Mommy, how does Jesus get into my heart?" A relative at a funeral falls apart, clings to us, and says, "I wish I had a faith like yours." A neighbor's child confides he is taking drugs and knows God can help him clean up his life, but he doesn't know how. Or a friend simply inquires, "Can you help me to know God for myself?"

What do we do? Hand the rod hastily to the pastor or church professional? Advise the inquirer to buy a good book that once helped you? Tell him or her to watch a great television evangelist? Or just "chicken out" and tell the seeker to go home and pray about it?

Now, all of the above may be helpful, but could it just be that *you* are supposed to land the fish all by yourself? If Jesus Christ is living in you and it's His job to win souls, then I suggest you take a deep breath and bring in your fish! As my friend once told me, "You can do it!"

But it's important to remember that you can never lead others to Christ unless you first know Him for yourself. We can learn that from the life of Peter. We meet Jesus and He gives us a new name. Right away our character begins to change. Then, when He calls us, we must be ready to leave our nets of habit and sin and follow Him out into deeper water to become "fishers of men." And going deeper involves obedience, "followship," possible suffering—but also, of course, the sunrise possibilities of breakfast with Jesus.

WORKSHEET

Chapter 2

I. Share some influences that led you to put your faith in the Christ, the Son of God.

II. Becoming a Christian presupposes change in our characters. Read the following passages and then answer the questions. (If you are in a group, divide into twos to discuss the questions and then share your answers with the whole group.)

1 Peter 2:9–20
1 Peter 3:13–17
1 Peter 4:1–6

a. Make a list of the differences Peter expects that Christ should make in our lives.
b. Try to put these differences in your own words. What specifically could such changes mean in terms of your everyday life?

III. PRAYERTIME: Praise God for one thing you learned today. Then pray to God for:

New converts at home and abroad
New programs to catch men and women
Your friends who need to find Christ
Yourself as you try to be a "fisher of men"

Chapter 3

RINGS

Mark 1:30–34

Simon's mother-in-law was in bed with a fever, and they told Jesus about her. So he went to her, took her hand and helped her up. The fever left her and she began to wait on them. That evening after sunset the people brought to Jesus all the sick and demon-possessed. The whole town gathered at the door, and Jesus healed many who had various diseases. He also drove out many demons, but he would not let the demons speak because they knew who he was.

Mark 1:30–34

Peter's Wife

God uses many sharp tools to craft us after His image, including the rings of our closest relationships. Peter, I believe, found that to be so. For Peter was not alone in learning lessons about the Lord Jesus. Those nearest and dearest to him had their own "close encounters of the best kind," too. Andrew met Jesus first, and then it was the turn of Peter's wife and his mother-in-law.

I have discovered you cannot know Jesus without wanting to make Him known, especially to those you love. When I found faith in Christ, I wanted the whole wide world to know about it! My mother and father, sister and friends, colleagues and workmates were each treated to a very inadequate but very enthusiastic account of my brand-new experience with God.

After all, if you have found the cure for cancer, you want to tell the world! I believed I had found the cure for a cancer much more deadly than the physical variety. Sin had eaten the souls of men away, and Jesus could heal the malady. It amazed me that the newspapers were not full of the glad good news, but I intended to put that right.

Peter, having been introduced to Jesus, quite naturally sought to involve the Lord with the rest of his family.

It happened this way: Peter's mother-in-law was sick. The disciples told Christ about her, and He went at once to Peter's home and healed her. Immediately she got up and saw to their needs, demonstrating clearly the full extent of her miraculous recovery.

We don't know if this was the first time the women in Peter's life had met Jesus. If only more had been said about that! I can't help wanting to know what sort of a women they were, particularly Peter's wife. Did she approve of Peter's involvement with Jesus? Did she object to the Lord's coming into her home and calmly walking off with her husband for three long years? Did she feel sorry for herself, or was she glad to pay the price of being an evangelist's wife—left without a husband, income, and all?

We do know that Peter's wife became a believer in Jesus, because the Bible tells us so. Paul, vindicating his ministry to his critics in 1 Corinthians 9:5, refers directly to Peter's marriage when he says, "Don't we have the right to take a believing wife along with us, as do the other apostles and the Lord's brothers and Cephas [Peter]?"

Heirs Together

We can also assume that Peter's marriage became a strong Christian partnership, and that it probably had a lot to do with shaping his life and ministry. For in his first Epistle he speaks eloquently about two married believers being heirs together of the gracious gift of eternal life. He obviously believes that Christian marriage is nothing less than a divine calling. The Living Bible renders it this way: "You [two] are partners in receiving God's blessings."

What a sad thing it is when only one partner in a marriage relationship is a receiver of God's blessings! If the spiritual part of us is the deepest part, why should we know each other at shallower levels than we need to?

How important it is, therefore, to choose a marriage partner who really knows and loves the Lord! So often, women say to me, "I am dating an unbeliever, but I am hoping to lead him to Christ." But the Bible warns us specifically against being "yoked together" with unbelievers (2 Cor. 6:14). In fact, Paul says, "Do not." If we insist on doing what we should "do not," then there's no point in praying about it. You don't bother praying about disobedience.

I am not saying we should not pray for the unbeliever's salvation; of course we need to do that. But perhaps the best thing we can do for such a person is to get out of the way and let God work in his or her life. Pray the Lord will send someone else along to bring the unbeliever to Himself. If we don't back off, how will we ever know if the person in question is really interested in commiting himself or herself to the Lord?

We won't know if the commitment is for His sake or for ours.

If, of course, you become a Christian when you are already married, that is a very different story. Paul, in fact, says in that case, "Do not seek a divorce" (1 Cor. 7:27), and urges the Christian partner to try to win the unbelieving partner to Christ. Peter was already married when he met Jesus, and we do not have the biblical information to tell us who found faith in Christ first—he or his wife. But we do know they counted themselves "heirs together" in Christian partnership.

I remember deciding as a young Christian that if I could not find a man who was a lover of Jesus, then I would not be a lover of any man! The whole concept of a shared ministry for God excited and challenged me. I couldn't think of anything more worthwhile than serving the Lord Jesus as a team. I found a verse in Joshua that said, "As for me and my house, we will serve the Lord" (24:15, KJV), and I determined that if I ever married, my husband and I would be a "we" and not a "he" and a "me"! I told God that if He gifted me with a believing partner, then I would not stand on the sidelines of my life, applauding my husband's exploits for God. As our rings would show our vows to serve each other, so they would show our commitment to serve Him together.

It was this personal sense of calling to serve the Christ I loved that has remained with me all of my life and has been an integral part of Stuart's and my marriage commitment to each other. And the evidence is that Peter and his wife were together in their calling and commitment to His cause.

A Hospitable Partnership

Not only were Peter and his wife partners in belief and commitment; they were partners in receiving others into their home and lives. When you inherit God's blessings, you find out you also inherit God's friends! As soon as Peter began to help Jesus get His work done, he found himself surrounded by a motley crew of lepers, paralytics, tax collectors, and sinners (Luke 5). He learned that receiving Jesus was one thing; receiving Jesus' friends was sometimes quite another!

Yet, the principle of Christian partnership is quite straightforward: hospitality becomes a way of life, a natural mindset. Peter and his wife learned this lesson early in their life of discipleship—and in a somewhat dramatic fashion.

It happened the very same day Peter's mother-in-law was healed. And it had been a full and memorable day for them all—starting out with worry and sorrow and culminating in the emotionally draining events of Jesus' miraculous touch and the older woman's full recovery. All of this was more than enough drama for one family in one day, but it turned out to be only the beginning. In the evening of that day, we are told "The whole town gathered at the door" (Mark 1:33)!

News spread quickly in those days, and someone had let it be known that Jesus of Nazareth was at Peter's house. So after the sun set, believers in Jesus began to arrive. There were lepers who believed He could make them clean, demon-possessed people who longed to be released from their torment, and a trail of sick folk brought by relatives desperately believing in a last chance.

And what of Peter's wife? How must she have felt about this intrusion on their privacy? She must surely have been tempted to think that the world should wait its turn!

And that raises another question. Did Peter's wife have the gift of hospitality? In truth I do not know, but I don't really think it matters whether you do or you don't when the whole town is gathered at your door! When that happens, you cope the best you can. You share what you have, and you get involved.

We must be careful to differentiate between the gift of hostessing and the gift of hospitality. The word *hospitality* means "the love of strangers," and that is one of Jesus' basic commands—not just a special gift for some. The Lord told His disciples to love the unlovely, the outcasts, the widows, and the lowly. For His sake, we are to make friends with those to whom we would not naturally be drawn. For as the Lord Jesus said, "If you love those who love you, what credit is that to you? Even 'sinners' love those who love them" (Luke 6:32).

The thing that was to make the world sit up and take notice

of Christianity was seeing the way that Christians loved each other. Jews and Greeks, slaves and freemen, men and women, in fact, people who "naturally" struggled to treat each other properly were to be transformed by Christ's love to consider others better than themselves (Phil. 2:3). They were to lay down their very lives for each other (John 15:13).

But loving fellow believers is one thing; loving unbelievers is another! Jesus addressed this issue, too. "God so loved the world that he gave his one and only Son" (John 3:16). Again the Scriptures say, "God demonstrates his own love for us in this: While we were still sinners, Christ died for us" (Rom. 5:8). Notice it says "while we were still sinners"—not "once we became saints!" Jesus told us to love the world as He had loved the world, and He promised to give us the Holy Spirit to help us to do it! It is the Holy Spirit who puts His love in our hearts for those we find it difficult and sometimes even impossible to love (Rom. 5:5)!

To experience individually and then together a love for total strangers—hospitality—is part of what Christian partnership is all about. And it is God who works that miracle in our hearts as we get to know and love Him better every day. Paul instructs the elders of the church to practice hospitality (Rom. 12:13). And since this injunction appears to be made to men and not to women, the apostle most likely does not have the gift of hostessing in mind.

In other words, all of us who are called to be believers are equally called to be receivers—men and women alike. Fortunately, Christ never calls without providing the wherewithal to perform that which He demands, and we need to remember that. If you happen to have those marvelous hostessing gifts, then that's a real plus. But if not, with His help you'll learn to muddle through anyway!

When Stuart and I married, he was a banker and I was a teacher in the British school system. We set up house in Manchester, and soon God gifted us with a beautiful child, David. In those days, young people gathered in coffee bars in droves, and there was one such meeting place right outside our house—"The Cat's Whisker."

Stuart traveled all week on business and was away most weekends preaching as a lay minister. That left me with plenty of time on my hands to think about doing something to reach those exciting young folk literally on our doorstep. However, I seemed to have lost my nerve. So one Friday I trained a few willing college kids to evangelize and sent them over the road to do what I was afraid to do myself!

Watching from my "safe" retreat across the street, I saw my little trained preachers panic as a fight broke out. The owners of the coffee bar tipped everyone out onto the street and closed up for the night! Then it was my turn to panic as I saw the mob move over the street to our house, invited by my intrepid team!

An incredible cast of characters invaded our home. They sprawled up the stairs and into the kitchen and den, the living room, and even the bedrooms! Having triumphantly brought me a net full of fish, my novice fishermen announced with relief that if everyone would shut up, "Jill" would speak to them.

That was a moment! I remember thinking, "This is ridiculous! If I tell these kids about Christ, they will think me a fool!" At once a verse popped into my mind from 1 Corinthians 1:21 that reminded me it was "by the foolishness of the preaching" that He would save some. So I just set about telling anyone in that mob who would listen about a God who was real; a Christ who had died; and a Holy Spirit who could impart faith, hope, love, and Jesus Himself to their human hearts.

The house was still packed at midnight with questioning, argumentative, skeptical kids. My husband, coming home very late from a preaching engagement, couldn't get into his own house. Eventually a youth with his long hair dyed in extraordinary colors opened the door a crack, said, "Sorry mate, there's no room," and shut the door!

"The whole town" gathered at our door that night, and Stuart and I were never the same again. I tell you, it mattered not whether I had the gift of hospitality! When people know Jesus is in your house, they will beat a path to your door—not necessarily to see your drapes or enjoy your home cooking, though both undoubtedly create a comfortable atmosphere to help people listen and learn, but primarily to meet Jesus!

Stuart and I both discovered that day, as God gave us a taste of Holy Ghost hospitality, that the love of strangers was truly planted in our hearts. "The one who calls you is faithful and he will do it" (1 Thes. 5:24).

Since those early days, our home has always been like Piccadilly Circus, and I have been able to learn a few of those hostessing tips that have helped me to do a better job with the practicalities. But I have also discovered that, even though I do not have the gift of hostessing, there is all the more need for me to "practice hospitality" as the Bible tells me to do (Rom. 12:13). And practice certainly makes better, if not perfect!

It's a huge release to know you don't need to be Ms. Perfect Hostess before you invite anyone into your home. I have observed that many church people have been really reluctant about using their homes for the Lord because they don't think the furniture is nice enough—it doesn't match—or they feel awkward because they can't do gourmet cooking. Well, join the club; I have felt that way, too. But when I discovered that people wanted to spend time with me, not my furniture, and to eat the bread of life, not my questionable baking, I was home safe. This has not meant I cover my furniture with dropcloths and poison my guests; on the contrary, I have worked very hard at making the most of what we have and have even learned to make a mean apple pie. But I also try to remember that it's Jesus they want and Jesus they need and Jesus they come to see! When someone's marriage is falling apart, it matters not that my sofa needs recovering. When a child has been discovered taking "crack," a distraught parent won't be interested to see how I set the table. And when an empty, hungry person wants a spiritual answer, he or she won't be looking at the pile of wash on the floor I haven't had time to do.

I learned to open my door at all times of the day and night and go right on doing what needed to be done. I would say to the bunch of teenagers that "just dropped by" when I had the baby in the bath, a toddler toddling into trouble, and soup boiling over on the stove: "Hi, come in—can I ever do with a hand!" Then I would give the wet baby to one of them to dry, ask another to stir the soup, and attend to my toddler while we chatted away. At other times I'd say, "Sure, you can come right in—you don't mind if I get on with this pile of ironing while we talk, do you?"

Oftentimes, I noticed that if the people saw I didn't stop everything because they had arrived, they felt a lot more comfortable about "intruding."

Obviously, you can't continue to bake if your visitor is having hysterics. But practicing hospitality means having an open home—not one that has "hours" like the post office.

Entertaining Angels

This does not mean we will not struggle with the challenge of it all. Even quite recently, I found myself resenting some "strangers" Jesus sent along to our home. I was busy arranging for a family reunion. Two of our children are married, and we all live far away from each other, so it is no small feat to bring us all together for family time. But I had somehow managed to get it all arranged, and we were to meet for three short days. Having accomplished my goal, I busied myself with the arrangements. Then I received a letter from some missionary friends asking us to invite their children over on that very weekend! I happened to know the children had friends who would also want to come along.

I found my mother-heart rebelling. "Lord," I complained, "why that particular weekend?" Then I began to bargain: "I tell you what. I'll have them for a week in the summer instead!" But those youngsters didn't need to come in the summer; they needed to come that weekend, and this left me with no option. So I prayed, "Please, Lord, don't let them ever know I am reluctant to have them come!"

Now, that was the best I could do at the time, so you can imagine my chagrin when I read Peter's words in 1 Peter 4:9: "Offer hospitality to one another without grumbling." To help me understand the verse, I looked it up in another version. It said, "Be hospitable to each other without secretly wishing you hadn't got to be!"

I got the message. I really believe some have entertained angels unawares. And maybe I was one of those people, as on that occasion a visiting stranger turned out to be a huge help to one of our children, who was struggling with some big decisions that had to be made that very week!

A hospitable lifestyle will require us to make sure people know we are available to them. Do we invite lots of people over to our house? Is ours the home that kids naturally love to come to after school?

This is something for each set of Christian partners to pray about. Ask God to give you opportunities to house strangers. Let your pastor know you would like to have visiting missionaries or other guests to stay. Be alert to needs in your community.

Not long ago our church hosted a conference. We appealed to the congregation for housing for the delegates. One young married couple told us they had had a wonderful experience housing missionaries from Zambia. I happened to know they have a very tiny house and only one bedroom. "We hired two beds and turned our living room over to them for the week," they explained. You see, it can be done!

The housing of guests was very important in the life of the early church as by and large the inns were not very respectable places for Christians to stay. Then, open homes were very necessary. Today, even though the Holiday Inn is just around the corner and the need is not so obvious, the opportunity hospitality affords us is a precious one that shouldn't be missed. One obvious benefit to our family has been that our children have had a chance to be part of the action, because the action happened right in their home. The influence of a changed life or of one of God's special people who has lived with us for a while has been very far-reaching.

Of course the hospitable lifestyle will force you to be flexible—and for very organized people this can be difficult. Flexibility is an art to be learned. It is the art of leaving things undone, of realizing people matter more than things, more than schedules, and even more than our own plans for the day. We need to ask God to build us like the skyscrapers are constructed in California—tall and straight, but with flexibility built into every joint! That way, when the earthquakes come, we won't collapse.

Jesus always had time for people, even when His own plans were interrupted. Once when He had received some bad news and all He wanted to do was get away for some peace and quiet, He was met by five thousand people. A multitude of need faced Him, and He calmly took care of it. The Bible says that when He saw them He was "moved with compassion" and cared for them (Mark 6:34, KJV). The Greek word translated "moved with compassion" means "convulsed." Are we convulsed with compassion when we are met by a multitude of need? In my experience, the multitude never picks a convenient time, because real need is usually an urgent affair that can't or won't wait!

For a husband and wife to be hospitable together means their partnership will be enriched. Peter and his wife came to realize that this was Jesus' way of life, the lifestyle the Lord prescribed for all His followers. Listen to the apostle Peter: "Offer hospitality to one another" (1 Peter 4:9–10). In other words, "I never grudge a meal or a bed to those who need them!"

Priorities of Christian Partnership

But some of you may object and ask, "What is the cost of such commitment? How will my children react when they are constantly being turned out of their bedrooms for some stranger or visiting pastor? And what of the marriage partnership itself? Surely we need to protect our relationship from intrusion from the outside world. And just how are we going to meet the needs of others if our own needs aren't being met?" Good questions. Let's try and find some answers. What does the Bible say and what does the Bible mean when it says it?

As far as I can see, it is extremely dangerous to be too dogmatic about having a rigid hierarchy of priorities. I have heard sermons that have stated categorically "God first, family second, church last!" Then again an equally persuasive case has been made for "Family first, God second, church last." In fact the permutations are so varied the confusion mounts the more you read and study the subject.

Part of the problem lies in some very straightforward words and teaching of Jesus. For example, Matthew 10:37 says, "Anyone who loves his father or mother more than me is not worthy of me; anyone who loves his son or daughter more than me is not worthy of me." In another place, the Lord tells us that we cannot even be His disciples if we "hate not" our father and mother, spouse and children, brothers and sisters—yes, and our own life also! (Luke 14:26, KJV). How, in the light of these verses, can we talk about our number-one priority being to first meet our partners needs?

C. I. Scofield, commenting in *The New Scofield Reference Bible,* sheds some light on the problem by explaining the so-called "hate principle," when referring to Luke 14:26. "Terms which define the emotions or affections," he says, "are frequently comparative. Natural affection is to be, as compared with the Christian's devotedness to Christ, as if it were hate. See Mt. 12:47–50, where Christ illustrates this principle in His own Person. But in the Lord the natural affections are sanctified and lifted to the level of the divine love (cp. Jn. 19:26–27; Eph. 5:25–28)." In other words, we can never love others too much, but we can surely love God too little!

Jesus in effect told us that the new relationships of the kingdom or our faith relationships with other believers must take precedent over our natural relationships. Not only did He teach this, He modeled it. Once when His mother and brothers came to see Him, He was told that they couldn't get near Him because of the crowd. According to Matthew 12:46–49, He responded by asking, "Who is my mother, and who are my brothers?" Then, pointing to His disciples, He said, "Here are my mother and my brothers."

How difficult this must have been for Jesus' family! How hurt they must surely have been! Yet Jesus was modeling His own teaching—first the King, first the Kingdom, first the

King's kin! That is what we need to remember as we shape our priorities.

And yet, there has to be a balance. Remember that Jesus spent thirty years in Nazareth. After Joseph died, He surely would have acted as head of the home and provider for the family. He spent only three short years in the ministry. Then again, we see that Jesus did not abandon His duty to His mother. Even on the cross, He gave her into John's care and keeping.

It must have been a sharper sorrow than even the soldiers' spear that His own brothers were not there to take Mary home with them. But in that particular situation Jesus' hands were tied—or, to put it bluntly, pinned into place by a hammer and nails! He could not do those things He must have longed to do for the one He loved better than life. At Calvary, "first the Kingdom and the King's kin" meant that the King had to let someone else minister to the people He loved most.

And therein lies the key. One day, "first the King" will mean one thing; the next day it may mean something else. A friend of mine who is a single missionary in Asia had a wonderful life as a career missionary translating the Bible. At first her family were well and cared for. But as the years passed her mother declined to the point that she needed constant attention. So for awhile, "first the King" meant my friend stayed home for an extended furlough to look after her. Later, it meant arranging for that beloved mother to be cared for in a home by strangers.

"First the King" means different things at different times where a family is concerned. It makes sense to realize that balance will only be achieved as we stay as close as we can to the King! "Lord, what wilt Thou have me to do today" must be a continual prayer. The pressures of figuring that one out will necessitate good communication with God, as well as with each other.

How real and vital is our prayer life? Do we understand that God will speak to us through His word and that His Spirit will interpret the meaning if we diligently study and ask for enlightenment? Our personal walk with the Lord is absolutely vital in our quest for right priorities. And each partner in a marriage needs to maintain his or her own vital link with God; it should not be left to one or the other. This way there is "double surety" in the decisions that are made about priorities. You will find that, as you ask God for the answers to "what comes first," He will be more than willing to reveal them to both of you—a great "checks and balances" system!

A Personal Gethsemane

You may also find that the answers you receive may mean you will experience a personal Gethsemane. Like Peter you will find a model in Jesus who prayed, "Not my will, but thine, be done" (Luke 22:42, KJV). It may mean a personal Calvary as well—dying, for the kingdom's sake, to your own desires to care for your own. But it will certainly also mean a personal Pentecost, which will provide the power you'll need to put others before yourself.

In the Book of Acts, we see the apostles living in community with the infant church. Acts 9:2 indicates there were women among them. So I feel certain that Peter's wife was with her husband and that they labored side by side for Jesus "as the Spirit enabled them" (Acts 2:4). And so He will enable us as we labor together in Christian partnership. He is the One who walks by our side, meets us around the corner of tomorrow, and enables us to be obedient.

Let me try to illustrate this. For Stuart and me, "first the King" has meant many different things at many different stages of our relationship, in many different seasons of our lives. At one time, it meant Stuart's being away on the King's business for months on end. We had three small children and worked for a youth mission. "How can Stuart fulfill the biblical role of a father and be away all the time?" someone asked me. "How can he fulfill the role of evangelist and be home all the time?" I replied. "First the King" for me during that period meant staying home and being Mom and Dad for our three lively youngsters.

Then again, there came a time that "first the King" meant

putting our children first. It was primarily for their sakes that we moved home and family to another country to give them a more stable teenage life. Situations change, we change, ministry changes, needs change, and for each couple there is a unique dynamic. So communication is vital—first with the King, and then with our partners.

How did Peter cope, I wonder? How did he and his wife figure it all out? For them "first the King" undoubtedly meant a good deal of loneliness for three long years as Peter traveled with Jesus. After that, it meant togetherness as they worked in the Jerusalem church. For both of them it involved a personal Gethsemane and Calvary as they were martyred for their faith—crucified, so tradition tells us.

There will be a different hierarchy of priorities for different people. What a freeing concept this is! And we are freed not to be selfish, but rather to determine His will and way for our family moment by moment and day by day!

Guidelines for Husbands and Wives

How are marriage partners to work together? The Bible gives specific guidelines—several of which come from Peter himself.

The husband, Peter says, will need to figure his wife out. "Husbands, in the same way be considerate as you live with your wives, and treat them with respect as the weaker partner and as heirs with you of the gracious gift of life, so that nothing will hinder your prayers" (1 Peter 3:7). In other words, he is telling the men to respect their wives' weaknesses and to honor their strengths.

The wife will need, as Paul puts it, to be nourished and cherished "just as Christ does the church" (Eph. 5:29). The man must be responsible to help her discover and develop her talents and gifts, and he will also answer to God for the way he has "cherished" or protected her as she does discover them. Some think the verse is saying that because of a woman's sexual makeup (this word "vessel" in the original Greek is used in a sexual sense in 1 Thess. 4:4), she is particularly vulnerable and may tend to "overtax" or "overload." So the husband will need to make sure she is not taking on too much.

Once again, each wife is different. Think of a wife as a boat. The Maker alone knows the capacity of the craft. For this reason He has put a "waterline" around our personalities, just as there is a waterline around a boat. If we are learning to know each other thoroughly as marriage partners, we will understand that not to be loaded with any responsibilities at all will be to be unfulfilled, while to be totally overloaded will mean we'll sink without a trace! There have been many times in my life when all that can be seen of me is my little white distress flag waving feebly above the waves!

I thank God for a husband who is my "boat inspector" and has figured me out! He does respect my weakness and he does honor my strengths. As Peter suggests, he has made sure I have had ample opportunity to fulfill my role as a wife and mom and also to exercise the spiritual abilities he has seen in me. As Peter says in 1 Peter 4:10, "Each one should use whatever gift he has received to serve others, faithfully administering God's grace in its various forms."

Sometimes we overload our own boats, and at other times other people overload them for us. There is so much serving to do, and I sometimes try to do it all. At one point I took on a "cargo" of meetings that was far too heavy to carry. They all looked fine on the calendar when I accepted the invitations and wrote them down; after all, most of our schedules look pretty empty a whole year ahead. But when I actually got there, heavy problems I could not possibly have anticipated were waiting for me. I had overloaded. I didn't know what to do. Once more I had allowed my heart to rule my head.

You can't just unload such cargo either. If people have planned to have you come to their town and have spent a year preparing for it, you have to go and fulfill your obligations. In that particular instance, it was my husband and children who helped me by unloading some of the burdens at home so I didn't sink. The Bible says we are to bear our own burdens, but it also tells us to bear one another's burdens.

If the husband's job is to respect his wife's weaknesses, honor her strengths, and above all to love her deeply (1 Peter 4:8), then what about the wife's responsibility?

Peter lays that out very clearly. She is to have a servant spirit (1 Peter 3:1), a sweet spirit (v. 4), and a strong spirit (v. 6). She will need the courage to do what is right, perhaps in the face of much criticism. "Do what is right and don't give way to fear," Peter exhorts us. Right from the start of our marriage, there was absolutely no doubt in our minds that God had called Stuart and me to a rather unusual partnership and given us a rather unusual calling to rather unusual people! And yet mature believers never stopped criticizing us for our ministry. I had to be strong and overcome my fear—not only of the loneliness, pressures, and dangers of our work, but also of what other Christians thought about us and what they said about the way we "should" be doing the work and bringing up our family. I believe Peter and his wife would have understood our dilemma!

Quite frankly, I wrestled more with fear of other Christians' disapproval than with anything else. Some people are so quick to "know it all" and tell others how they should be living the Christian life, ordering their family relationships, bringing up their children, and conducting their ministries that they forget Jesus told us not to judge—that we should cast out the plank in our own eye before we start scratching out the speck in our brother's!

How often have I heard mature Christians waxing eloquent about clergy and missionary parents who ruin their children by neglect—by sending them off to boarding school or not spending any time with them. Now, I know some children of couples in full-time ministry don't make it, but then some children of car salesmen and lawyers don't make it either! I would want to know the dynamics of the relationship of a particular troubled family before I would even dare voice a suggestion as to what may have gone wrong. If the father had been at home in a "normal" situation, for instance, would he have done any better? Was his relationship with his wife such that he would simply have "escaped" by staying late at the office or going on business trips instead of on missionary trips?

Missionaries are ordinary people living in extraordinary circumstances—called to do extraordinary tasks with very little help and less than adequate resources. By and large they do a wonderful job, but they would be very much more effective if we who support them (and therefore think we have the inalienable right to criticize them) would pray more and try to think of practical ways to unload their boats for them once in a while! It is a very heavy burden to be told continually, "Your children will never make it—they will grow up to reject the Lord!" Sometimes I used to get the feeling that those giving us this "loving council" would almost be glad if that *did* happen to our kids—because then their opinions would be vindicated!

Even now, with our three children grown and in ministry, I have on occasion been told, "Well it was obviously the grace of God, despite what you did to them, that brought them through!" Now undoubtedly there is a lot of truth in that; it was certainly by the grace of God that they turned out so well! But I have come to realize that no one does it all right—and no one does it all wrong, either! We mustn't demand that all Christian families live according to this formula or that, but try and encourage each family to find out His formula and fulfill it!

A Unique Grouping

When I was a student, I took a pottery class. We had to cast five pots, and each one had to be different. It took us all semester to do it, and then we were told to arrange the pottery in a grouping. This was a very important part of the course; the way that the group was arranged was supposed to show the pots off to their best advantage.

I was amazed how long it took me to move those five pots around till I found the "right" position for them. Well, I *thought* I had found the right position!

When the examination began, the visiting teacher—a master potter—took endless time looking carefully at each of our works of art. Each student watched anxiously to see what the teacher would do. Sometimes she would leave the vessels as they were. At other times, she would totally restructure the group. When she came to mine, she took the two largest pots and moved them apart from each other. Then she set the little pots in between. Everyone smiled in delight. The two big pots looked so much better with a little bit of space between them!

I have often thought about that examination and would almost call it prophetic! Stuart and I are so strong individually and have similar gifts. We have been told our individual and corporate ministries are seen to their best advantage with a little bit of distance between them. The Master Potter knows how best to bring glory to Himself by the way He orders our lives. We *must* ask Him.

One day I will meet Peter's wife. I can't wait! Perhaps she will share with me the struggles of her life with Peter. He probably wasn't the easiest man to live with! But then, for that matter, a shy girl from the Galilee country region was probably not the strongest candidate for public ministry and martyrdom! They would have to work it all out together with the Lord.

But we mustn't copy or compete. Peter and his wife were one couple, Stuart and I are another, and you and your partner are still another. The rings that symbolize our relationships are undoubtedly different from the rings that symbolize yours, be they rings of friendship, family, or marriage. Peter and his wife, however, give us the urgent reminder that whatever the cost of Christian partnership down here on earth, the time is short, and the job of telling the world about Jesus Christ before it is too late *must* be done (2 Peter 3:10–11). We will have all eternity to be together. A little bit of cost and commitment to Him now is really a very, very small thing in the light of eternity!

WORKSHEET

Chapter 3

I. Review the meaning of *hospitality*.
   a. How does one develop the "love of strangers"?
   b. Read the following verses. What is their significance in terms of developing the gift of hospitality?
      Romans 12:13
      Hebrews 13:15–16
      1 Peter 4:9
   c. What practical thing have you learned about hospitality that you can put into action?

II. Review the following verses and then answer the questions in light of them:
      Matthew 10:37
      Matthew 12:46–49
      Luke 8:19–21
      Matthew 6:33
   a. What does it mean to put God first?
   b. What doesn't it mean?

III. Read 1 Peter 3:1–7.
   a. Make a list of the qualities commanded for both husbands and wives.
   b. Which qualities in your list do you need to work on and why?
   c. Which ones do you need to encourage in your spouse and how?

IV. PRAYERTIME:
   a. Praise God for families and loving relationships.
   b. Think of *one* relationship that has helped you. Praise God for it.
   c. Spend a few minutes in silence thinking about how to prioritize your family time. Then pray about it.
   d. Pray for Christian leaders and their families.
   e. Pray for troubled families.

Chapter 4

TOWELS

John 13:4–12

So [Jesus] got up from the meal, took off his outer clothing, and wrapped a towel around his waist. After that, he poured water into a basin and began to wash his disciples' feet, drying them with the towel that was wrapped around him. He came to Simon Peter, who said to him, "Lord, are you going to wash my feet?" Jesus replied, "You do not realize now what I am doing, but later you will understand." "No," said Peter, "you shall never wash my feet." Jesus answered, "Unless I wash you, you have no part with me." "Then, Lord," Simon Peter replied, "not just my feet but my hands and my head as well!" Jesus answered, "A person who has had a bath needs only to wash his feet; his whole body is clean. And you are clean, though not every one of you." For he knew who was going to betray him, and that was why he said not every one was clean. When he had finished washing their feet, he put on his clothes and returned to his place. "Do you understand what I have done for you?" he asked them.

John 13:4–12

The Order of the Towel

The Savior's attitude of humility startled the disciples. After all, He was their Master and Lord. But toward the end of His ministry, as they went up to Jerusalem for the Passover feast, they knew He must not only be followed and obeyed, but emulated as well. To live as Jesus lived however, was not the easiest thing in the world to do. To enter "the order of the towel," for instance, was an unexpected challenge for the disciples—especially, I suspect, for Peter!

But then, humility is a tough assignment for all of us! Which of us wakes up in the morning racking our brains for new ways to be humble and serve others? Usually our waking moments are filled with thoughts about ourselves and who is going to serve us. "Why doesn't someone else get breakfast ready for a change," mutters the hassled mother. "Has my shirt been ironed?" demands the senior high kid—who only slung it in the basement yesterday. The grade schooler wants to know who is taking her to school when she could have been up early enough to take the bus and save someone the trouble!

It was at the Last Supper that Jesus modeled the lesson of servanthood for His disciples and for the rest of us. The order of that night's events differs in each of the Gospels, but it is generally agreed that the background for "the lesson in humility" was a dispute among the disciples about greatness (Luke 22:24–27).

A few weeks prior to this event, the disciples had been walking along the way with Jesus. Lagging a little way behind the Lord, they had argued about which of them was the most important (Luke 9:46–48). Jesus, "knowing their thoughts," had taken a little child and set him in their midst as an example of one who was "least" among them. And then He had commented, "He who is least among you all—he is the greatest." Jesus told them in no uncertain terms, "If anyone wants to be first, he must be the very last, and the servant of all" (Mark 9:35). He even went so far as to say that unless their hearts were humbled as the heart of a little child, they would not even be able to enter the kingdom of God, much less be honored in it (Matt. 18:3)!

Jesus' message was clear, but apparently the disciples didn't "get it." They continued to compete with one another over who was greatest. Even the mother of James and John got in on the act according to Matthew 20:20–28. She had taken note of the fact that her boys were always being singled out, along with Simon Peter, for special treatment, so she took it upon herself to ask for some future privileges for them. She actually requested of Jesus that her two sons would sit at His right and left hand in His kingdom (v. 21).

Well, you can imagine that once the rest of the twelve heard about that, they were pretty "indignant with the two brothers" (v. 24). So Jesus patiently called them together and tried again! "You know," He said, "that the rulers of the Gentiles lord it over them, and their high officials exercise authority over them. Not so with you. Instead, whoever wants to become great among you must be your servant, and whoever wants to be first must be your slave—just as the Son of Man did not come to be served, but to serve, and to give his life as a ransom for many" (vv. 25–28).

All of us struggle with putting others first in our lives. I well remember a time when our three children beautifully illustrated the point. Our eldest, David, was thirteen at the time; Judy was eleven; and Peter, the youngest, was nine. Peter had recently experienced a growth spurt and suddenly, to his amazement and delight, he found himself on eye level with his siblings. He had believed up to now that his lot in life was to suffer humbly and quietly, his brother and sister having the obvious advantage of age, height, and experience. After all, he was youngest and shortest and knew what was good for him! But now an unexpected turn of events had taken place. He discovered he was big enough to hold his own—yea, more than that, to give as good as he got!

The two older children marched him in to me one day as I prepared lunch in the kitchen. "Mother," David exploded, "something is terribly wrong with Peter."

"Yes," Judy interrupted, "we don't know what's happened. He thinks he's as important as we are!"

"Of course he is as important as you are," I remonstrated.

"How can he be?" David asked, quite exasperated. "He's number three!"

Now, we may laugh a little at such childish talk, but don't let us laugh too loud or too long, or we may find the laugh is on us! How often do we look at others and ask the same exasperated questions: "Who do they think they are? They obviously think they are as important as I am!" Oh, yes, the human heart has much to learn from Jesus!

A Lesson in Serving

Jesus had tried hard to get over to His men the principle of humility—a "me last" instead of a "me first" perspective—but His efforts hadn't done much good! Now, on the very night in which He would be betrayed, they were at it again. The Lord decided it was time to stop talking and show them what He meant. As William Hendriksen says, "It was in the midst of such men—men with the *so big* attitude of heart, men with Judas the traitor in their midst—Jesus was to set an example of humility and service" (*New Testament Commentary Series: John,* Baker Book House, 1961, p. 229).

The "so big" attitude of heart stops many disciples of Jesus from attaining the greatness of the humble mind that honors God, esteems others better than themselves, and wins men to Christ! We see it in our churches when people use manipulative politics to make sure pet candidates become elders or deacons. We hear it as leadership is criticized and motives of envy are revealed. We observe its carnage among choir members jostling to sing the big solos or women trying to control other women in the church circle.

There is no end to the possibilities the church provides for disciples to fight over the "greatness" issue. But one thing we can know—as we put our gloves on, call on our supporters, and wait impatiently for the bell to ring to bring us out fighting—it all brings grief to God's heart!

So on that last night, supper being over, Jesus "got up from the meal, took off his outer clothing, and wrapped a towel around his waist. After that, he poured water into a basin and began to wash his disciples' feet, drying them with the towel that was wrapped around him" (John 13:4–5). Some have suggested that such a drastic action symbolized the greatest of humility, for it meant taking on the garb of a slave. One who laid aside both upper garments, as Jesus did, was left wearing only a loin cloth, and such a garment denoted the very lowest class of servitude.

To have so big a God attend the feet of such small men in such a way was surely an example of perfect grace and humility. But then the servant spirit is a gracious spirit! Grace has been defined as "doing something for someone who doesn't deserve it one little bit." When Jesus washed the feet of His disciples, He washed feet that didn't deserve it one little bit!

Dipping the cloth in the bowl of water, Jesus washed the feet of all the disciples—even Judas! And the amazing thing to me is that He did it all *knowing* what these men were about to do to Him!

The Bible says, "for he knew who was going to betray him" (John 13:11)—namely Judas! But not only did Jesus know Judas's feet were about to run to perpetrate dire treachery; He also knew that Peter's feet would soon "follow . . . afar off," carrying him to a place where he would deny his Lord with oaths and curses (Mark 14:54, 71, KJV). Jesus knew that the feet of the ten would soon run away from their Master's predicament. He was well aware, we are told, that the Father would soon "strike the shepherd, and the sheep [would] be scattered" (Mark 14:27).

Knowing, however, made no difference in the way Jesus served His disciples. Knowing all things, He still knelt down and washed their feet. What grace! And how we need this grace of God to operate in our own lives!

I can think of many instances in which I have seen the humility and grace of Jesus in operation. For example, I know a woman whose husband left her and their three young children for another woman. The wife and little ones joined our fellowship and began to try and pick up the pieces of their shattered lives. Then one day the mother came to see me. Through her tears, she told me that her ex-husband and his girlfriend had begun to attend the church! What was more, the couple had actually signed up for a Sunday school class that she was team-teaching! How could she possibly face them, much less serve or minister to them? What grace she was going to need to "wash the feet" that were running away with her hopes and dreams!

As I watched that woman struggle through the ensuing weeks with that horrendous challenge, I witnessed the way the Lord Jesus helped her react to those people with Christlike tenderness. It was a wonderful thing to see the evidence of the gracious spirit of the living God in the life of a woman under such trying circumstances.

Doing the Dirty Work

The disciples of Jesus had walked through dusty, dirty streets to get to the upper room. Their feet, clad in the open sandals of the day, would have been dirty, hot, and smelly by the time they all arrived. The usual custom was that the host would see to it that a servant or a woman washed the guests' feet. Seeing that the host on that particular occasion had omitted to do his duty, one of the disciples should have performed that task. But none of them, alas, were willing to go to such lengths for each other.

The squabble that had broken out among the disciples had probably risen in connection with who was to sit next to Jesus at the table. The seats with most prestige were those reserved next to the honored guest. When Jesus perceived what was happening, He apparently decided it was high time for a "servant spirit" lesson.

Jesus wanted us to know that a servant spirit is not the same as "servile" spirit. It is not to be confused with groveling or whining or fear. The fact is, as far as God is concerned, greatness is measured with the yardstick of service.

The disciples, upset and angry at being pushed out of the

"best seats," were far more concerned about their perceived rights than their obvious responsibilities. But service says, "I have no rights; my joy is to do those things I need not do because 'I may,' not because 'I must'!" Service, in fact, cultivates the "may I" rather than the "must I" attitude.

As the disciples ate their food—their feet unwashed, feeling undoubtedly uncomfortable—each one was probably hoping someone else would get up and do that dirty job that nobody ever wants to do! "Must I?" they kept saying to themselves. Or, "Why me? Why not him? I knew Jesus first—the ones who came to know Him last should do it." Or, "I'm older, it's the young people's work." But whatever was running through their minds was rudely interrupted by the incredible sight of Jesus the Messiah, King of Kings and Lord of Lords, stripped to the waist and pouring water into a bowl, girding Himself with a towel and kneeling at their feet asking, "May I?"

Watching Him, Peter must have suddenly become aware of the suffering that service entails. Implicit in the whole concept of service modeled so exquisitely by Jesus are the ideas of cost, giving, going the extra mile, even dying. And Peter was definitely not into dying—yet!

Stuart and I were privileged to work with Major and Mrs. Ian Thomas for many very happy, hectic years. We lived in a big castle in the English Lake District that had been turned into a youth facility in order to house camps and short-term Bible schools for young people. The castle was beautiful to look at, but hard to transform into twentieth-century usefulness. Still, the youth lent their energy and time and all their enthusiasm to the endless projects of this transformation—and Major Thomas, the leader of the mission, worked right alongside them.

Major Thomas had been decorated for bravery in World War II. One of the decorations was the D.S.O. and another the T.D.—the letters standing for Distinguished Service Order and Territorial Decoration. But someone on the staff kiddingly told him we were sure it rather stood for "Dirty Shirt on Tinkering-down Drains!" For Major Thomas believed in a Christianity that is not afraid to get its hands dirty, and his rugged, manly, attractive modeling of this principle won many a rugged, manly, attractive kid to Christ.

To serve Christ does not exempt us from the nitty-gritty doings of life. So often we think of Christian service as something clean, spiritual, and "above" all the practical, ordinary—even distasteful—things that "someone has to do." Yet Jesus showed us otherwise on that night when He took up the towel.

Learning to serve in practical ways has always been something of a challenge to me. God has graced me with speaking gifts, and I could quite easily fill every waking moment with speaking engagements. And yet I have always tried to balance those gifts with service action.

Keeping an open house has been one way I have deliberately invited a lot of hard work into my life. It takes hours to clean the house and plan the meals, to shop and run here and there making guests comfortable and happy.

Another thing I have done to make sure I had plenty of practice washing dirty feet was to involve myself with "need" ministries. In the past, I got involved with poor families, helping to clean old people's tenement houses, painting at a Chinese mission in the inner city, and gutting out condemned buildings for youth facilities. At one point we bought an old four-story grain warehouse and began to turn it into an outreach post for the town. I well remember finding a dead cat in the basement and being very tempted to tell one of the kids to get rid of it, but I managed to take care of it myself. I even helped to pass buckets of concrete down an old, rickety ladder for hours on end.

I wanted to wash dirty feet—to follow Jesus and not leave those tasks to other people while I sat on a throne and pontificated about the servant spirit! For the servant spirit is a spirit that insists we serve at the lowest level. A true servant goes to all lengths, even suffers if need be, to render service to the Master!

Jesus, the Suffering Servant

Jesus had once asked the disciples, "Who do people say the Son of Man is?" And they had answered, "Some say John the Baptist; others say Elijah; and still others, Jeremiah or one of the prophets." "But what about you?" Jesus asked. "Who do you say I am?" Simon Peter answered, "You are the Christ, the Son of the living God." Jesus was delighted and replied, "Blessed are you, Simon son of Jonah, for this was not revealed to you by man, but by my Father in heaven" (Matt. 16:14–17).

Well, for once Peter seemed to have got it! Jesus *was* the Christ, the King that was to come, the One the prophets had predicted would deliver Israel from the yoke of oppression. But actually Peter, as we shall see, had only got half of it. For Peter was thinking Romans, not redemption! He had not yet grasped the fact that suffering was part of Jesus' saving mission.

"From that time on Jesus began to explain to his disciples that he must go to Jerusalem and suffer many things at the hands of the elders, chief priests and teachers of the law, and that he must be killed and on the third day be raised to life. Peter took him aside and began to rebuke him. 'Never, Lord!' he said. 'This shall never happen to you!' Jesus turned and said to Peter, 'Out of my sight, Satan! You are a stumbling block to me; you do not have in mind the things of God, but the things of men'" (Matt. 16:21–23).

Peter hadn't got this part! He was still struggling to put together the two Old Testament concepts—the King who would be like David and Isaiah's suffering Servant. It would take the cross and the resurrection and the endowment of the Holy Spirit at Pentecost for Peter to finally understand that Jehovah's suffering Servant and Jesus of Nazareth were truly one and the same figure. Then he would be able to write, in a letter to young believers, that "he himself bore our sins in his body on the tree, so that we might die to sins and live for righteousness; for by his wounds you have been healed" (1 Peter 2:24).

Like Peter, we tend to be slow to comprehend the suffering angle in Jesus' message. To know Christ the King is to enjoy the benefits of the kingdom He invites us to share. But to know Jesus as Savior also involves taking up our crosses and following Him. He did not tell us to take up His cross and die on it—He was the only one who could do that—but to take up our own crosses and die to whatever would prevent us from serving our God and our world.

But we don't want to hear that. Our problem is we are happy to identify with the King—but not the Servant. To identify with a popular, colorful, "on the way to the top" religion sounds like something we'd all like. But to identify with a crucified man requires us to take a bowl of water and wash someone's dirty feet—and that's something else altogether! We may be tempted to think that when we are born free people there is absolutely no necessity to become slaves. I would agree—unless you are a follower of Jesus.

We are so "self" conscious these days. We tenderly save ourselves from anything that would tire, stretch, or challenge us. *Conservation* is the key word. "If I served Christ in this or that capacity," we say, "it would make me feel 'demeaned' or demand too much of my time and energy. Therefore, I must not do it, for God surely wants me to love myself."

Yes, God does want us to love ourselves—but that doesn't mean coddle ourselves! One of my favorite old hymns contains the words, "Let me burn out for thee, Lord Jesus." But nowadays I can open Christian magazines that seem to advertise a plethora of seminars set up for American Christians on such subjects as "How to Avoid Burnout"! What happened to us? To serve is to spend ourselves, not to save ourselves. Personally, I don't want to get to heaven having spent myself as sparingly as possible, but would rather "*always* give myself fully to the work of the Lord, because I know that my labor in the Lord is not in vain" (1 Cor. 15:58, paraphrased, emphasis mine).

We need to know that this whole lifestyle of servanthood may make us unhappy now and then. Being Jehovah's suffering Servant no doubt made Jesus unhappy!

One of the problems was that He knew too much! He knew His time was up; John 13:1 tells us that "Jesus knew that the time had come for him to leave this world and go to the Father." That alone was enough to make Him sad; thirty-three is a very young age to face death. I remember my husband saying to me on my thirty-third birthday, "You've had as much time as Jesus had!" That was quite a shock. I felt so young, as if I had only just begun.

The Lord must also have been unhappy on other accounts. Certainly He must have been frustrated with His disciples. During His last days on earth, I'm sure Jesus would have had His mother and His family in mind; perhaps He wanted to spend time with them. But this was His last chance to instruct the twelve men who were to lay the building blocks of the doctrine of the Christian faith. So He chose to spend His precious time with the disciples—and they were griping and grumbling about who could sit next to Him at dinner! Talk about frustration! Jesus must have suffered to know that their minds were operating at such a base level. What incredible restraint was displayed when He said gently to them, "I have much more to say to you, more than you can now bear" (John 16:12).

Most of all, Jesus must have suffered deep unhappiness because He loved so deeply. The fact is that the nature of love is to suffer, and the greatest suffering is often caused in the area of our closest relationships. We suffer because we serve those we love, and when our love is rebuffed or rejected and our service derided or ignored, sadness will inevitably be the result. In his book *The Four Loves,* C. S. Lewis says, "Love anything and your heart will certainly be wrung and possibly be broken!" The alternative, however, is no alternative. To "conserve" rather than to serve is to become isolated, cold, hard—to die a little bit as a person day by day!

Even if love brings us suffering, in the end, it is also love that motivates us to serve. Jesus, "having loved his own who were in the world . . . now showed them the full extent of his love" (John 13:1). A loving spirit loves to the end. Atlas, it is said, had the world on his shoulder, but Christ had the world on His heart! When that happens, then you "lay down your life for your friends." And as Jesus explained, there is no greater love than this (John 15:13). Perhaps that is why the apostle Paul said on one occasion, "I die every day" (1 Cor. 15:31), meaning one of the first acts of discipleship is to surrender oneself to any and all possibilities of self-giving instead of self-serving.

This will require dependence on God—not self-confidence, but God-confidence. Peter was a pretty self-confident character. The idea of "meekness" would be a hard one to sell to the rough, tough fisherman. I'm sure he didn't like the idea one little bit. But that is probably because, like a lot of other people, he thought meekness meant weakness! Not so! The Greek word denotes "controlled strength." Imagine a powerful horse responding to a signal from its rider and you have some little idea of what the word means.

Like Peter, I was a pretty self-serving person before I found Christ. Then, as He began to rein in and control my selfish actions, He motivated me to get involved in loving, practical "doing" for others. This was certainly a revolutionary idea for me. And it needed to be worked out in the context of my life, too. Life was very hectic, married as I was to a young traveling preacher and finding myself responsible for three lively children under the age of six. I could hardly wait for my husband to walk through the door at night to present him with the long list of all the tasks I had saved up for him.

As I grew as a Christian, however, the whole concept of love and service became a challenge I couldn't ignore. I found myself driven to ask the question, "What can I save him from?" rather than "What can I save for him?" A Christian servant actively thinks of ways to save those he loves time, energy, and work.

Not long ago, after I had shared this particular concept at a meeting, a rather angry young lady wrote to me. "The servant spirit you suggest," she wrote, "is a slur on your own sex. It is an attitude that binds and cripples women." I wrote back to her, pointing out that I tried to serve others not because I was a woman, but because I was a disciple who happened to be a woman. I quoted Jesus in John 13:14: "Now that I, your Lord and Teacher, have washed your feet, you also should wash one another's feet. I have set you an example that you should do as I have done for you." What is more, I said, most of the time such a lifestyle gives me great joy. I found Jesus' words to be true: "Now that you know these things, you will be blessed if you do them" (v. 17).

A Picture of Sanctification

There was, however, a lot more to the lesson Jesus acted out that night than simply an example of love and service. Jesus used His symbolic action to teach a deeper and most significant truth concerning the need for sanctification. *Sanctification* is that work of God within the heart of the believer that has to do with making him or her like Christ.

The picture Jesus painted was a graphic one, and we need to understand it against the culture of the day. A man living in that particular place and time would take a bath before leaving for supper. He would obviously not then be in need of another one on arriving at the banquet hall. Only his feet would need washing.

When Jesus came to Peter and knelt at his feet, Peter withdrew with the horrified protest, "Lord . . . you shall never wash my feet." Jesus answered, "Unless I wash you, you have no part with me." "Then, Lord," Simon Peter replied in typical fashion, "not just my feet but my hands and my head as well!" (John 13:8–9).

It was at this point that Jesus referred to the custom of bathing, pointing out the necessity for only the feet to be washed. He then carried the symbolism in His action into the spiritual realm by referring to Judas, who was not *spiritually* clean.

Later that night, Jesus prayed after this fashion: "My prayer is not that you take them [his disciples] out of the world but that you protect them from the evil one. They are not of the world, even as I am not of it. Sanctify them by the truth; your word is truth. As you sent me into the world, I have sent them into the world. For them I sanctify myself, that they too may be truly sanctified" (John 17:15–19). Jesus was thinking about our dirty spiritual feet—the feet of the twelve disciples and the million and twelve who would believe in Christ because of those disciples.

Think of it this way. If we have become a follower of Christ, He has forgiven us all our sin. We are clean—we have "bathed." But we have been left in this world—this dirty world—to be witnesses to the truth. Jesus comes to us at the end of the day and kneels down to wash our feet. How do we respond to Him? Do we snatch our feet away, preferring them dirty or ask one of the disciples to clean us up? There will probably be as many reasons for refusing cleansing as there are people who need it!

Cleansing, after all, is the great want of the human race. Spiritual purity is the essence of divine fellowship. If He washes us not, we have no part with Him. As John puts it in his first Epistle, "the blood of Jesus, his Son, purifies us from every sin" (1 John 1:7).

Our basic relationship with God depends upon our spiritual birth, just as our relationship with our earthly father depends upon our birth. Our ongoing fellowship with Him, however, depends upon our behavior. Once we have been justified—made "just-as-if-I'd-never-sinned," we are born again into God's family. Our fellowship in that forever family, however, will depend upon our acting responsibly about our relationships. And day by day, we will need to let Jesus remove the street dirt—the defilement of our sins against each other. As someone has aptly put it, "Pride must sit still as a naughty child and have its feet washed and wiped." It's hard to admit we have been wrong, yet no one else can admit it for us. "Humble yourselves, therefore, under God's mighty hand," exhorts Peter, of all people (1 Peter 5:6). For Peter, who at first did not want to accept his Lord's example, is able to say in the end, "Be shepherds of God's flock . . . not lording it over those entrusted to you, but being examples" (1 Peter 5:2–3).

So cleansing becomes a choice—our choice! Just as justification is a choice for the sinner, so sanctification is a choice for the saint. Peter had an option. He could say, "No, you shall *never* wash my feet!" or he could say, "Go ahead, Lord Jesus." That crucial option is ours as well.

Where does this daily cleansing take place? In our hearts—in prayer. In a quiet moment after a defiling thought or word or deed. Perhaps in the evening at sunset, or maybe in the morning in the cool of the day.

What form does cleansing take? Our part is confession—the exposure of the defiled part of our lives to God. We must prostrate ourselves in God's presence as Isaiah did when he exclaimed, "For I am a man of unclean lips" (Isa. 6:5). And then God will do His part, just as He did with Isaiah. For once Isaiah had confessed, an angel flew with a cleansing coal from the altar of God, laid it on Isaiah's mouth, and said, "See, this has touched your lips, your guilt is taken away and your sin atoned for" (Isa. 6:5–7). Our part is confession; His, the cleansing.

Whatever form our confession takes, it must be specific and honest and particular. Perhaps we will have to say to Jesus, "Oh, my mind!" or "my hands!" or "my nasty ego!" or "the sense of my own importance!" And that confession must be accompanied by a willingness to put out of our lives everything that we know is sinful.

In other words, confession is not just regret or remorse, or simply admitting we have done wrong. Rather, confession says, "Jesus, I have to admit I have been walking in some pretty dirty places. Please wash my feet and give me the power not to walk that way again."

Shortly after I became a student, I received an intriguing invitation to attend a rather risqué party. I was pretty sure of the sort of things that would be going on there, and I turned to my Bible to find a directive. I discovered one almost immediately: "Remove thy foot from evil" (Prov. 4:27, KJV), and again from Peter: "I urge you, as aliens and strangers in the world, to abstain from sinful desires, which war against your soul" (1 Peter 2:11).

I had been to such parties before I became a Christian, and so I knew there was no way to walk into that situation without walking out of it with dirty feet! So I prayed that God would give me the power to walk "after the Spirit," not "after the flesh" (Rom. 8:1, KJV). He helped me say no to the invitation, to remove my feet literally from walking into that building where the party would take place. And He also enabled me to take the consequences of my actions in terms of the broken relationships that ensued.

So I kept my feet clean in that instance. Yet no sooner did I walk "right" in one situation than I walked "wrong" in another! There has never been a perfect day in my life. Every day I've heard the water poured into the bowl and seen Jesus addressing my dusty, dirty, smelly feet!

Faithful Friends

One of the most exciting things about this passage of Scripture is the repercussions of Jesus' teaching. "Do you understand what I have done for you?" Jesus asked them. "You call me 'Teacher' and 'Lord,' and rightly so, for that is what I am. Now that I, your Lord and Teacher, have washed your feet, you also should wash one another's feet" (John 13:12–14). The Lord not only meant for us to practice loving, humble practical service; He hoped we would catch the vision of spiritually washing each other's feet. In other words, we are to aid each other in being clean Christians.

In the early days of my Christian faith I was aided in my efforts to be obedient and "walk after the Lord" by some wonderful helpers. The girl who led me to Jesus helped me to study the Word of God. She pointed out Psalm 119:105: "Your word is a lamp to my feet and a light for my path." She explained that I would need a lamp to help me to avoid the mud puddles of life and that the Bible was the lamp I needed. And I found that to be true the moment I began to read it.

Being young and romantic of heart, I fell in love not long after that. The object of my affections was a personable young man who lost no time in sweeping me off my feet and proposing marriage. I wrote to Janet—the girl who had led me to Christ—about it. She replied at once, asking me one very pertinent question: "Is he a Christian?" I had to reply, "No."

Instead of coming down hard on me, she sent me two passages of Scripture, deciding to allow the Word of God to do the necessary work in my life. I read 2 Corinthians 6:17–18 with interest: "Therefore come out from them and be separate, says the Lord. Touch no unclean thing, and I will receive you. I will be a Father to you, and you will be my sons and daughters, says the Lord Almighty." I had never come across these verses before.

But it was the first chapter of Daniel that really got to me. As I read the story of Daniel, a young person like me who was tempted to eat the king's meat—a delectable food—I noted the fact that he refused it. The reasons for this were that the meat had been offered to idols and Daniel, being a kosher Jew, knew he could not eat it without defiling himself (Dan. 1:8).

In a flash I knew Daniel's temptation was mine. Bob was delectable and, quite frankly, looked good enough to eat! But I knew I would be "defiled" if I continued my relationship with him, simply because such a relationship was forbidden in Scripture. Hadn't I just read it with my own eyes? Jesus had prayed, "Sanctify them by the truth; your word is truth," and here it was doing its challenging and commanding work in my heart. After a long prayer time and many tears, I resolved not to put my relationship with God in jeopardy because of my relationship with Bob. I would not eat the "royal food and wine." That night I withdrew from the friendship. After a while I was able to sit down and write a note of thanks to Janet. And I asked God to help me to do for others what she had done for me!

Perhaps you face a similar situation. You are well aware you need to remove your foot from evil. Maybe you have been rationalizing your sin and calling it something else—love, perhaps! Maybe you have fallen in love with someone who is clearly "out of bounds" as far as Scripture is concerned. Perhaps that person is married already, or not a committed believer in the Lord Jesus. Confess it, let Jesus wash your feet, and purpose in your heart never to walk that path again.

Maybe you think you would never smile again if you passed such an opportunity by. Not so. John tells us, "If we walk in the light, as he is in the light, we have fellowship with one another, and the blood of Jesus, his Son, purifies us from every sin" (1 John 1:7). And we will discover that cleansing brings its own contentment. Jesus said, "Now that you know these things, you will be blessed if you do them," and He meant exactly what He said. "Weeping may endure for a night"—as we struggle to be obedient or to repent and confess a sinful action. But oh, does "joy [ever] cometh in the morning" (Ps. 30:5, KJV)!

"Blessed" means to have a real sense of God's approval in your heart—one that brings a warmth of fulfillment and assurance of Divine favor. He smiles, and our spirit smiles back!

It is a humbling thing to be used in someone else's life to aid them in becoming a clean Christian. Yet it is the huge privilege of every one of us who follow Jesus. We are called to be a kingdom of priests (1 Peter 2:9). But such ministry cannot be accomplished by proud people! We must be walking in the light of His word ourselves, before we can ever have such a ministry to others.

Peter never outgrew his need for daily cleansing. He argued with Paul, made some serious errors of judgment, backed away from his convictions in the face of opposition, and no doubt struggled with his temperament all the days of his life. But I believe Jesus and Peter met regularly over that bowl of water and that Peter learned the hard way the order of the towel. Listen to him: "Clothe yourselves with humility toward one another, because, 'God opposes the proud but gives grace to the humble'" (1 Peter 5:5). *Clothe* is a word picture denoting the tying on of a towel around the waist of a servant. Now where do you think Peter got *that* idea?

I see You smiling while I strip my
  carnal clothing off.
I hear You laugh as water splashes
  in the bowl.
I look above and catch Divinity's delight—
  I kneel and seek with washing word
    to cleanse a soul.

Yet, I could never dare to dress in
  servant's garb
Unless I first have known Your
  cleansing blood
Have fallen prostrate crying,
  "Mercy, Lord—
forgive my filthy feet their
  wayward road!"

So humble this high head
  till low it bows
before a cross where
  sacred head hangs low.
Teach me the lowly secret of
  the Christ,
Then help me hear You say,
  "My servant—go."

Oh, Lord, may I always be known by my uniform—the towel!

WORKSHEET

Chapter 4

I. Read John 13:1–17. If you had been Jesus, which part of these events would have been hard for you, and why?

II. Read Isaiah 42:1–7. Make a list of the characteristics of "The Servant of Jehovah."

III. Read John 1:5–10. What is this passage saying about our daily walk and the need for cleansing?

IV. Read each of the following passages. (If you are meeting in a group, divide into twos to read the Scriptures and discuss the questions. Then share your answers with the whole group.)

1 Peter 2:13–20
1 Peter 2:21–25
1 Peter 3:13–17

a. If we are to follow in His steps, what may we expect?
b. What one thing strikes you most about being a suffering servant?

V. Can you think of one person God is sending you to serve this week?

a. What one practical thing can you do for him or her?
b. When will you do it?

VI. PRAYERTIME: Read 1 Peter 4:12–19.

a. Praise God for the example of Jesus as a servant.
b. Pray for your own servant attitude.

Chapter 5

ROOSTERS

Luke 22:54–62

Then seizing him, they led him away and took him into the house of the high priest. Peter followed at a distance. But when they had kindled a fire in the middle of the courtyard and had sat down together, Peter sat down with them. A servant girl saw him seated there in the firelight. She looked closely at him and said, "This man was with him." But he denied it. "Woman, I don't know him," he said. A little later someone else saw him and said, "You also are one of them." "Man, I am not!" Peter replied. About an hour later another asserted, "Certainly this fellow was with him, for he is a Galilean." Peter replied, "Man, I don't know what you're talking about!" Just as he was speaking, the rooster crowed. The Lord turned and looked straight at Peter. Then Peter remembered the word the Lord had spoken to him: "Before the rooster crows today, you will disown me three times." And he went outside and wept bitterly.

Luke 22:54–62

A Dark Night

When you say "roosters," you say Peter—that is, if you have been to Sunday school and church and know the Gospel story.

A very short time before He died, Jesus warned Peter that he would disown Him three times before the rooster crowed (Luke 22:34). When Jesus was arrested by the chief priests and officers of the temple guard, all the disciples fled. But as they led Jesus away, Peter followed at a distance (v. 54). Entering the high priest's courtyard, the big man mingled with the crowd to see what was going to happen. Challenged by a servant girl about his relationship to Christ, he denied it vehemently, saying, "Woman, I don't know him." Three times this happened. Then the rooster crowed, just as Jesus had predicted it would. And Peter "went outside and wept bitterly" (v. 62).

It's a dark night indeed when we disown the Lord—when we fail Him. And there are many ways this can happen. Perhaps, like Peter, we have followed well, and then we fail to follow on. Actually, the Bible doesn't say Peter failed to follow; it says he failed to follow closely. When we follow Jesus closely, we can hear His voice and sense His presence, but when we deliberately put distance between us, we hear only the clamor of the opposition and lose sight of God Himself! It is then that we panic as Peter did, and we end up failing both Jesus and ourselves.

If we are to keep near the Lord, we must keep praying. Earlier that night, Jesus had taken His men to the beautiful garden of Gethsemane, His favorite retreat. Jesus particularly asked Peter, James, and John to watch and pray with Him as He battled out His last agony of submission to the Father's will. The Lord knew the cross was just around the corner of tomorrow.

But the garden was so peaceful it was hard to believe there was a need to watch and pray. The smell of the flowers and the soft, sweet night breezes lulled the tired disciples to sleep.

Very few of us pray *before* trouble comes. Most of us wait

until the soldiers arrive on the scene, the arrests are made, the trial is in progress, and the cross is in sight before we get around to praying. But the problem is that no one prays well on the way to the cross! The praying must be done beforehand, when Gethsemane is peaceful and the trauma is yet to come. If we fail to be fortified by prayer, we will not do well when Judas arrives—or when we find ourselves at a charcoal fire, surrounded by a hostile crowd.

Before—not after—is the critical time to pray. Therefore, says Jesus, "Why are you sleeping? . . . Get up and pray so that you will not fall into temptation" (Luke 22:46).

Peter, however, slept while his Master prayed (Luke 22:45). And so he also resisted while his Master submitted (vv. 47–51); sat down with his Lord's enemies (v. 55); and denied the Lord, the faith, and the brotherhood (vv. 57–60). Then the rooster crowed—startling Peter into a guilty awareness of what he had done.

Have you ever heard the rooster crow? I have. And I suspect most Christians know the awful feeling that comes when we know we have failed the Lord.

"I Can't Believe I Did That"

Before I committed my life to Christ, of course, I didn't really worry about failing Him. But once I understood that Jesus had not failed me but had given His life that I may succeed in being the human being He had created me to be, it began to be very important indeed that I please Him.

At first, however, the possibility of ever disowning Him appeared to be extremely remote—almost unthinkable. After all, hadn't He promised us all the power we would ever need for obeying, all the words we would ever want for explaining our faith, and all the help we would ever require from people in the church if our feet should ever falter? I was like a cocky rookie on the baseball team. I couldn't imagine ever letting the side down.

Of course, Christianity and baseball are not to be compared. A rookie who fails the team will eventually be traded, and Christ never trades us, even if we are having the worst season of our lives! He promises for those who come to Him, "No one can snatch them out of my Father's hand" (John 10:29). And He assures us that whoever comes to Him, "I will in no wise cast out" (John 6:37, KJV).

I once saw this verse illustrated for children. The speaker held a quarter in his hand. He stood the coin on its rim and cupped his palm to hold it upright. "You are safe in the Father's hand," he said. "When an enemy comes"—and he used his free hand to represent an adversary—"the Father keeps you safe"—he closed his hand over the coin. "Sometimes," he continued, opening his fingers and letting the coin fall over, "you will fall down—but," he finished with great triumph, "you will never fall out!"

We all looked at that little coin lying flat in the man's large and adequate hand, and I'm sure old and young alike were thinking of the many times we had messed up one way or another. "Thank you, Father," I whispered, "that failure is never final for the Christian. You help us to stand up again even if we have fallen flat on our face!"

But again, the fact that Christ never lets us down doesn't mean we don't let Him down. At some point in our lives, despite our cocky self-confidence, we all fall flat on our faces. Which brings us back to Peter. What happened when he fell over? Well, one thing is certain: he didn't fall out of the Father's hand. I'm quite sure, however, knowing Peter, that he was very angry with himself for failing the Lord. I can imagine him weeping bitter, angry tears of self-recrimination and saying over and over again, "I can't believe I did that!"

After all, hadn't Peter boasted to Jesus in front of everybody, "Even if all fall away on account of you, I *never* will" (Matt. 26:33)? Oh, but we must never say never. That's an awfully stupid thing to say—because we cannot know when we may find ourselves in circumstances that are too much for us.

As Peter found himself surrounded by Jesus haters and realized that the jealous leaders interrogating the Lord were out to finish Him off, he must have also realized that was no place to be if you were wearing country clothes and had a strong

Galilean accent! It was certainly not the safest place in the world if you had just cut off a fellow's ear and discovered you were warming your hands at the same charcoal fire as one of his relatives (John 18:26)! So Peter tried to be as unobtrusive as possible as he mingled with the officials and servants warming their hands at the fire—but his speech betrayed him (Matt. 26:73).

As the accusations of his complicity with Jesus mounted, something snapped. And Peter—or rather Simon—reverted to "before Christ" behavior, cursing and swearing and denying he had ever known the Lord! Then the rooster crowed, and Jesus turned and looked straight at Peter, as if to say, "Self-confidence dies when faced with a cross! For that you need Me!"

No wonder Peter wept bitterly. What remorse he must have experienced! I can just hear him saying over and over again, "I can't believe I did that! I can't believe I did that!"

I well remember a time when I felt just like that. When faced with a hostile group of acquaintances who objected to my refusing to drink with them and who wanted to know what made me think I was "holier" than they were, I was cowed into silence. I just couldn't seem to find the right words to give them a cheerful Christian reason for my changed lifestyle! Sometimes silence is as eloquent a denial as speech. I remember sitting miserably in a corner, watching my opportunity tiptoeing out the door and saying to myself, "I can't believe I did that!"—or rather, "I can't believe I *didn't* do that!" We can deny the Lord both positively and negatively, I discovered.

I can imagine King David's experiencing the same sort of thing as well. I'm sure he never dreamed of committing adultery and murder, but that was before he grew middle-aged and Bathsheba moved in next door!

Perhaps David and Peter and I had something in common; we had not prepared ourselves adequately for the force or size of the enemy! David was a great commander on the battlefield, but a terrible soldier when it came to resisting temptation. Peter was a great talker, but that was when his audience consisted of convinced soldiers of Christ and not rough soldiers of the temple guard. And I was a pretty good talker, too, until faced with the possibility of rejection.

Being a great talker doesn't necessarily mean you are a great walker. Followers falter and fall—even the best of them.

Our Adversary

If we are going to deal with failure *when*—not *if*—it comes we are going to have to know just *what*—or rather just *who*—we are up against!

When Jesus predicted Peter's denial, He told him, "Simon, Simon, Satan has asked to sift you as wheat. But I have prayed for you, Simon, that your faith may not fail. And when you have turned back, strengthen your brothers" (Luke 22:31–32). Who is this Satan Jesus was talking about?

He's been around a long while! He doesn't age; in fact, he's exactly the same today as he was in Adam's, David's, and Peter's time. He doesn't change, either, for a change denotes something better or worse. The enemy of our souls can't get any worse, and alas he can't get any better. This at least gives us a chance to understand his actions and perhaps study his strategy that we may be better prepared and "not be ignorant of his devices" (2 Cor. 2:11, KJV).

Satan is real. Those who imagine a little red figure in tights, brandishing a pitchfork with sinners dangling off the end of it, are way off track! Satan is a terrible being. Jesus believed in him and told us we had better believe in him, too. Peter was certainly thoroughly convinced of his existence and later gave us a very graphic, though figurative, picture: "Your enemy the devil prowls around like a roaring lion looking for someone to devour" (1 Peter 5:8). If we laugh at the very idea of such a spiritually evil animal prowling around our lives, then we will be easy meat. At least if we know he is a reality, we have a better chance of escape. Peter likened him to a hungry lion. The lion is the king of beasts, as Satan is the king of spiritual beasts.

I once heard about a young seminary student who was given a sermon to prepare. "Your subject is the devil," his professor informed him. When the time came to deliver his address, the young man stood up, cleared his throat, and began: "I know a good sermon should have three points, so here are mine. My text is 1 Peter 5:8. My subject is the devil. Point one: Who the devil is he? Point two: Who the devil isn't he? And point three: What the devil is he roaring about?"

The young man had three succinct points. We don't know what else was in his sermon, but we can follow his outline with profit!

Ezekiel 28:11–15 tells us who Satan *was.* He was the model of perfection who once was "full of wisdom and perfect in beauty" (v. 12). He was in Eden, the garden of God. Ordained and anointed as a guardian cherub, he was blameless in his ways until he fell from his position through pride. As a result, sin was introduced into the universe (Isa. 14:12–14).

Jesus gives us a sidelight on the situation in Luke 10:18: "I saw Satan fall like lightning from heaven." And Revelation 12:7–11 fills in a few of the details of his expulsion along with the angels that had joined in his rebellion.

Since then, Satan has made earth the scene of his relentless activity (Eph. 2:2). He wants the human race to be as he is and do what he has done, which is to rebel and fight God. He is prince of this world and is busy organizing earth's present system on the principles of greed, selfish ambition, and sinful pride.

The devil has many names. Among other things, he is called "our adversary," "the accuser of the brethren," "Satan," "Abaddon," and the "great serpent." He is real, and we'd better believe it! He is hungry, and we'd better heed it! And he is angry, and we'd better know it! He is particularly furious with believers in Jesus—especially those who are listening to God instead of listening to him!

Unfortunately, Satan is not a bad dream from which we could wake. He is not a prehistoric notion or a religious symbol. And he is certainly "roaring" about the place after us.

Now, *that's* scary! Just imagine if the head of a world terrorist organization targeted us and let it be known in the press that his agents were heading our way. How frightened we would be. I'm sure we would take all the necessary precautions we could to protect ourselves. We would be prayerful, watchful, and careful!

It's also scary because God has permitted Satan certain powers of sifting and testing the self-confident carnal believer. Remember, that's what Jesus told Peter: "Satan has asked to sift you."

When Jesus tells us that Satan has "asked" to "sift" us, that should strike far more terror into our hearts than any earthly terrorist's threat!

On the other hand, Satan does have to ask! That counters my fear and gives me confidence. God and Satan are not beings of equal force battling over my soul. God created Satan in the first place, and therefore the Lord is the greater power. The devil is permitted certain freedoms, but he has to ask before being allowed to tempt and try us.

We see this illustrated in the book of Job. Satan had to ask God to allow him to sift Job: "'Does Job fear God for nothing?' Satan replied. 'Have you not put a hedge around him and his household and everything he has? You have blessed the work of his hands, so that his flocks and herds are spread throughout the land. But stretch out your hand and strike everything he has, and he will surely curse you to your face.' The Lord said to Satan, 'Very well, then, everything he has is in your hands, but on the man himself do not lay a finger'" (Job 1:9–12).

Satan is limited in the amount of sifting he is permitted to do, and we need to realize the Lord allows tests and trials not to punish us, but to refine us that our faith may be proved. God's permissive will may be a mystery to us—if God loves us, why does He ever say yes to Satan? But at least it brings us a measure of comfort to know that the devil has to say "please" before being allowed to sift us through the sieve of suffering.

If we were more aware of just who we are up against, we may be persuaded to pray instead of falling asleep, to follow Jesus more closely and not let our "shield of faith, with which you can extinguish all the flaming arrows of the evil one," to tarnish (Eph. 6:16). After all, the devil's downfall is predicted through the seed of the woman—and that means Jesus (Gen. 3:15)! Satan's final doom in the lake of fire is ensured (Rev. 20:10).

Our Advocate

But who will protect us against these Satan's spiritual terrorist attacks? Will our prayers be enough?

No, they won't—but they will link us to the One whose prayers *will* be enough. He is our Advocate.

Jesus said, "Satan has asked to sift you as wheat. But I have prayed for you, that your faith may not fail." I'm so glad Jesus is praying for me—and that He knows exactly what to pray about. Aren't you glad He is praying for you?

So many times I get on my knees to pray for others and don't know what on earth to pray about. But Jesus is the expert on prayer. He always knows what it is we and other people need. He knew exactly what He needed to be asking on Peter's behalf; in fact, He had *already* prayed about it.

Not only that; He assured Peter of the answer—Jesus' prayers *always* get answered, of course. "*When* you have turned back," He said to Peter—not "*if* you have turned back" —"strengthen your brethren" (Luke 22:32).

Jesus expects us to fall prey to some of Satan's attacks. But when we do, He uses these sifting experiences in our lives to winnow out the carnality of our human nature till the pure wheat of Christian character is produced.

When Jesus prayed His great high priestly prayer in John 17, He asked the Father to protect us from the evil one, set us apart for Himself, unify us in love and bring us safely home to glory. But it all takes time! The next time you get impatient with yourself because your prayers for progress aren't getting answered, think about this.

Jesus' prayers were eventually answered for Peter, but not before terrible failure on Peter's part. The certainty that all things work together for the ultimate good (Rom. 8:28) helps us keep on keeping on at such times. The "ultimate good" is the glory in the end that Jesus has promised will be ours. The

Lord has already asked the Father to make sure we all arrive in heaven, pure at last. But it's the bit in between "here" and "there" that's the problem, isn't it? Jesus wants us to know He will give us the freedom to fail and also the faith to pick ourselves up, dust ourselves off, and try again. And this will probably go on until eventually we see Him as He is and be like Him (1 John 3:2).

Our Answer

Whenever we hear the rooster crow in our lives, we can know the Lord is prepared, has been praying, and is planning for us in love. Even if we are one step behind because we have been following from a distance, we can know He is already one giant step ahead of us.

For God's answer to the reality that we *will* fail Him from time to time is to turn our failures around! God organizes the circumstances around our failures to bring Himself honor and glory and to help us into a deeper relationship with Him.

There's a wonderful example of that in the Old Testament. Joseph and his brothers were not the best of friends. The older men were angry at their young brother. Their father favored him, and he hadn't helped matters by recounting strange, God-given dreams that set himself up and put them down.

But even though Joseph was probably unwise to tell them these things, he certainly didn't deserve the treatment he received! After they had put him in a pit while they debated the manner of his death and then sold him into slavery, you'd think Joseph would have had it with his brothers! (I know big brothers dream of putting little brothers in pits and selling them into slavery in Egypt, but few ever actually do it!)

God, however, cared for Joseph while he was in that foreign country. And eventually God brought him, after much suffering, into favor with Pharaoh. When Joseph eventually came face to face with his brothers again, they were at his mercy. He had been put in charge of the whole country, and they had come to beg bread.

What would you have done with the brothers? Joseph came

through with love, mercy, and forgiveness—and an assurance that God had been at work redeeming the terrible situation. "You intended to harm me," he told them, "but God intended it for good" (Gen. 50:20). Joseph knew that the Lord is quite able to use the most trying circumstances to eventually bring Himself honor and us blessing. God is sovereign and will work His purposes out. Joseph's brothers had failed miserably and treated Joseph shamefully. And yet God, knowing in advance what they would do, had met them on the other side of their failure with forgiveness and grace.

Joseph's story is a wonderful example of how the Lord can bring good out of our most dismal failures. But there is another point to be noted here—and it has to do with how we treat our brothers' failures.

Joseph didn't fail when it came to forgiving his brothers. Of course, he failed at other times in his life; after all, he was man and not God. But he didn't fail this time.

It would have been very understandable if Joseph had decided to get his own back. Perhaps that's what we would have done if we had been in his sandals. In fact, if there is one place we all need to be wary, it is in the area of our "brother relationships." But Joseph decided he was neither judge nor jury for his brothers; he would leave that part to God! Perhaps adversity had taught him a thing or two—such as the fact that he was only responsible for his own attitudes and actions, not those of other people!

That was a lesson Peter needed to learn! For Peter, looking around the circle of his brother disciples gathered for their Last Supper together, had been quick to judge them. "Even if all fall away on account of you," he had boasted to Jesus—giving the distinct impression he wouldn't be at all surprised if they did just that—"I never will" (Matt. 26:33)!

We fail God when we judge our brothers for their motives and actions—just as surely as we fail by denying Him. What others do is not our business. Whatever they do to us, our responsibility is to make sure we do not do it to them. We must treat them as Joseph treated his brothers and not "put them in a hole" or "sell them down the river" by some gossip or unkind word or deed.

If God handles our failures by turning them into opportunities for good, what is our part? What do we do when we have failed one way or another—when we have failed to witness or to be a good mother, father, brother, sister, or friend? What do we do when the rooster crows and we find ourselves saying, "I can't believe I did that"?

When failure comes, we must begin to handle the problems ourselves. And that means we will need to come clean and let Jesus help us handle our yesterdays, our todays, and our tomorrows.

Our Yesterdays

The most important thing to remember when we have failed is to come clean about our past inadequacies—to face up to what we have done.

When King David was confronted by Nathan, the prophet who exposed his great sin with Bathsheba, David at once acknowledged his failure: "I have sinned against the Lord," he said (2 Sam. 12:13). He could quite easily have made excuses and said, "It's my past that's responsible for my present behavior. My father sinned, and his sins affected me so much I just couldn't help myself—so it's really not my fault." And that would have been true! David's father, Jesse, was always leaving his youngest son out of things—treating him like the "runt of the litter." When Samuel the mighty prophet came to town, Jesse didn't even invite David to come from tending the sheep and join the party (1 Sam. 16:11)!

David could also have complained about how his brothers treated him. He could well have said, "They were always picking on me as if I was a boy—not a man—and it gave me such a terrible complex that I've been trying to prove myself ever since. In fact, that's exactly what happened when I saw Bathsheba—I had to prove myself a man!"

But David didn't blame his father, his brothers, or even Bathsheba for his failure; he accepted the blame himself. When faced with it, he said, "I have sinned."

When Jesus talked with Peter at the lakeside after His resurrection (John 21:15–17), He very gently took the apostle back to the point of his past failure and forced him to face it. For I believe that is what was happening in that well-known conversation where Jesus kept asking Peter, "Do you love Me?"

When the Lord asked that question, He used the Greek word for deep, sacrificial, unconditional love. Peter must have known He was really saying, "Peter, you boasted you would die for me, what do you say now?" For when Peter answered, "Lord, You know that I love You," he used a different Greek word for another kind of love.

"Lord, You know all things," Peter was saying in effect, "You're right; I claimed I loved You as deeply as You loved me, but now I know I must only be vaguely fond of You! I've failed You, Lord." Peter did not blame anyone else. He did not say, "Well, the rest of the disciples ran away and forced me to run away with them!" He "owned" the failure.

The morning that Jesus made breakfast for Peter over a charcoal fire (John 21:9–12), the acrid smell of the burning fuel must have brought to Peter a vivid reminder of another charcoal fire on another dreadful day already past. Have you ever had such vivid reminders of your failures? And do these reminders meet you at the most unexpected times in the most unexpected places?

When that happens, try not to push the memory away. Instead, face it, however painful it is. But then, once you have traveled back in memory, acknowledge your part of the action and ask God to forgive you once and for all.

I remember failing to speak about Jesus to a beloved and dying relative. After that, every time I went to a funeral and smelled the smell of death I would groan inwardly and murmur, "Lord, You know all things; You know how I failed You." Or the scent of lilies would do it—or maybe seeing the hunched back of someone's aged aunt being helped off a bus! Our senses can develop the picture, bringing the scene into sharp focus in the darkroom of our memories and presenting us with a clear reproduction of our past.

I had to work with such flashbacks, letting my mind work through those pictures and sharing them with the Lord Jesus. He never took my "photographs" away from me, but He did stop me from putting them in an album and reviewing them every minute of the day. And He forbade me to show them to every single person who came along! He simply assured me I had been forgiven and told me to remember that every time I needed to.

The sad thing is that the longer we have been Christians, the more trouble we seem to have even admitting we have failed Jesus. It's a bit like a basketball game. Have you ever watched a professional team playing a game with a rookie on board who has just come up from the college leagues? I have been struck with the difference between the rookie and the veteran.

Up and down the court they go until someone commits a foul. If the foul is called on the rookie, what does he do? Usually, up goes his hand to acknowledge it; "Sorry, ref!" he says ruefully. But it's a different matter if the foul is called on the veteran! He argues, scowls, towers over the ref, points to someone else, and is still protesting when the free throw is taken! Not all veterans behave like that, it's true. But alas, many of them do!

When I was new in Christ, my hand would shoot up quickly to acknowledge my fouls. But as I grew older in the Christian faith, I became far less sensitive to my own sin and found it a lot easier to blame the other players or even the Ref!!

Why, I wonder, is it so very hard for "veteran" Christians to admit wrongdoing? Perhaps it is because we are sons and daughters of Adam and Eve and we have inherited their attitude. Do you remember how Adam blamed Eve for giving him the apple and Eve blamed the serpent for offering it to her in the first place (Gen. 3:12–13)?

Whether we are "rookie" Christians or "veterans," the principle is the same—if we would deal properly with our failure, we need to know first what to do with our yesterdays. We must acknowledge the fouls and ask for forgiveness. Then we will have a chance to get on with the game.

Our Todays

Once we have confessed our past sin and allowed God to forgive us, we should take steps to live in our todays in a manner that will keep yesterday's guilt from paralyzing us. Having breakfast with Jesus each day will help! If we meet the Lord over breakfast, then again at supper (over that servant's washbasin of water), we won't go far wrong! It's what Jesus and I talk about today that will keep yesterday in its proper perspective.

Perhaps your marriage has failed. You have been carrying a huge load of guilt about it all. Yesterday is too painful to think about, so you have tried to repress it and put it out of your mind. But that hasn't worked. Perhaps someone told you to go back in memory, to admit the "fouls" you committed in your marriage and to hear Jesus forgive you for them. You did all that, and a measure of relief came. But even that didn't last.

In such a situation, perhaps it's today and not yesterday that's the problem. So try this: today when you meet the Lord, start saying thank you for the forgiveness of yesterday. Practice praise, and you'll find the memories will heal in the end. You will never be able to *forget* your yesterdays, but Jesus will help you to remember without becoming obsessed with your memories.

If you are a parent of teenagers, you probably know what it is like to have an argument with one of your children. (Maybe *battles* would be a more appropriate word!) Then sometimes a teenager will punish his or her parents by giving them the silent treatment. I have a friend who endured this particular situation for weeks with her teenager. This mother became obsessed with the problem. Every day she would wake up with that uneasy feeling that tells you something is out of place in your world! Then she would spend her waking moments—in fact, the rest of her day—remembering the row. She would go over and over the whole scene in her mind, blaming herself for more and more of it. She couldn't function in the home, at the office, or at church. Her todays were totally governed and controlled by her yesterdays.

The devil loves to see this happening. If he can only stop us from living today for Jesus, he's won—because he knows we only have today! He doesn't much care how he achieves his goal, but one of his favorite ways is to keep us saying "please forgive me" instead of "thank you"!

Our Tomorrows

And what about our tomorrows? Will failure in our past disqualify us for service in our future? Well, it didn't disqualify Peter! After he and several other disciples had spent a fruitless night fishing, they suddenly saw a man standing on the seashore. He called out to them to try casting their nets on the right side of the boat. They obeyed, and they caught an incredible number of fish.

"It's the Lord," exclaimed John to Peter, remembering another such miraculous incident. Peter jumped overboard and swam the intervening distance to reach Jesus. By the time the rest of the disciples arrived, dragging the nets with them, a time of reconciliation had taken place between Jesus and His subdued disciple (John 21:1–8).

After breakfast, the Lord and Peter took a walk along the shore of Galilee. There was much to talk about. The Lord had been asking Peter some pretty hard questions. He had helped him to travel back in mind to his painful yesterdays, to remember the humiliating moment when he had sworn he never knew his Master. Then, having forgiven Peter for his yesterdays, Jesus lit up his todays with promises for his tomorrows! "Feed my sheep, and my lambs," He said to Peter, focusing the apostle's eyes ahead of him to the task at hand (vv. 15–19).

Peter was overjoyed not to be disqualified from serving Jesus. Here was the Lord giving him a clear call to service. Peter—big-mouthed, boastful Peter—was happy beyond belief. The past faded, the present became a springboard for the future, and Peter couldn't wait to get on with it all!

Sometimes past failure clouds our futures with foreboding. Perhaps we have honestly tried to serve the Lord in the past and our efforts have ended up in one big mess. There were hurt feelings and broken relationships on every hand. Maybe we decided we would never try to do anything in the church ever again. I know folks who have gone so far as to withdraw their membership and refuse to worship with the Lord's people anymore. They sit at home and listen to tapes instead of identifying with a local body of believers. Sometimes it's so much hassle working with other Christians that it's a relief to withdraw.

Apparently the early Christians faced similar problems, for the apostle Paul admonished, "Let us not give up meeting together, as some are in the habit of doing, but let us encourage one another—and all the more as you see the Day approaching" (Heb. 10:25). We in the church are not to let others control or impede our progress, and we must not allow ourselves to stop us, either.

That day, as Jesus and Peter walked along the lakeside, Peter turned around and saw John following them. "Lord, what about him?" Peter asked Jesus. And Jesus replied, in effect, "Mind your own business, Peter, *you* follow me!" (John 21:20–22).

He was not telling Peter to "do his own thing"; there is no place for mavericks in the church of Jesus Christ. But He was telling Peter not to worry about his brothers or to let their triumphs or failures distract him from following the Lord himself.

Actually, Jesus had been telling Peter some pretty heavy things about his future: "When you were younger you dressed yourself and went where you wanted; but when you are old you will stretch out your hands, and someone else will dress you and lead you where you do not want to go" (John 21:18). He had been giving Peter a hint about the sort of death that Peter would endure.

Typically competitive, Peter immediately wanted to know if John's death was going to match up to his and how he would handle the test when it came! But the Lord brought His impulsive and inquisitive disciple back to his own responsibilities and told him he could safely leave John in His hands!

When Stuart and I worked among teenagers, I remember becoming overly concerned with their spiritual progress, especially as they began to leave school and go off to college. Would they go on with the Lord? I worried. What if they fell in love with someone who didn't love Jesus as they did? What would happen to them in later life? Would they live well and die well?

As I prayed about it all—or, to be more correct, worried about it all in prayer—I read John 21. I realized I had been asking the Lord the same question Peter had asked about John: "What about these kids?" He answered me as He answered Peter: "That's My business, not yours! You follow Me!"

In the end, we are only responsible for our own obedience. Of course, our lives are bound up with those we love—our nearest and dearest, or our colleagues at work or at church. And certainly our hearts will be touched by the sheep and lambs we tend. But our own following is quite enough for us to handle, as is our own failure! Our yesterdays, todays, and tomorrows are our prime responsibility—no one else's—and other folks' lives are their own. I came to realize it would take all of my time and energy to cope with the Lord's grand directives for my own life, and I must not allow the spiritual mercury of other people's lives to put my own temperature up!

After the Rooster Crows

Self-confident people like Simon Peter have marvelous potential for leadership. Yet their very strengths can also be their weaknesses. Peter learned the hard way that he should never say never. If he did, he was bound to hear the rooster crow!

Are you a self-confident person? Do you think you will never disown the Lord? Oh, our temptations will obviously not take place against a backdrop of charcoal fires, palaces, and roosters crowing. More probably, they will take modern forms, yet our temptations will be none the less compelling and frightening.

The devil has asked to sift us, and sift us he will—whether in office or home. May we be found faithful, whatever the cost. But if and when we fail, we can know that Jesus is our Advocate—that He has prayed for us. And after we are "turned back to Him," we will be able to strengthen our brothers and sisters with the encouragement we ourselves have found from Jesus—after the rooster crows!

I have found this to be true in my speaking ministry. People seem to respond when I illustrate Scripture teaching with personal illustrations that show my own failures. Not only do these simple words of testimony seem to "light up" some of the truths I'm trying hard to communicate; they also help people identify with me, and this in turn helps them listen. I have learned that people like a speaker who freely admits he or she doesn't have it all together. I see young mothers visibly relax when I share how I yelled at my children or panicked when my daughter went on her first date. People seem relieved to realize that the rooster has crowed many times in my life, and that some days I must have breakfast with Jesus three times before lunch!

I am convinced Peter was a lot easier to live with after his humiliating experience in the courtyard of the high priest's house. Of course, all the disciples had much to confess, for they had all forsaken Jesus and fled. But Peter especially, I am sure, was a chastened and much nicer man after the rooster crowed. Now, his fellow disciples would be ready and willing to listen to him. And I'm sure they never heard Peter say never again!

I'll never fail Him,
said Self-Confidence with intense pride!
I love Him! And when I love—I love!
I know what it is to be loyal to the people close to me!
THEN THE COCK CROWED. . . .
Self-Confidence hadn't understood how lonely she would feel
when her husband was out of town!
She'd only meant to have a business lunch
with the handsome young man in the office.

I'll never deny my Christian faith again,
Self-Confidence vowed, very much chastened.
Thank goodness, my marriage has been salvaged!
She took some Bible courses
so she'd know how to answer Temptation
when he came knocking at her door again.

She got A's for the course.
Now she was ready!
THEN THE COCK CROWED. . . .
Somehow she couldn't remember the Bible verses
when the young man kept saying such nice things
to her all the time. It was very flattering. . . .
After all, she was twice his age!

I'll never forsake Him again,
Self-Confidence swore to herself.
He can really rely on me this time.
I've learned my lesson—that's for sure!
Watch out, devil, here I come,
wielding my shiny little sword of self-sufficiency!
THEN THE COCK CROWED. . . .
And they took Jesus—
And crucified Him!

Self-Confidence died with grief.
Jesus, risen from the dead, visited her tomb.
Taking her hand, He lifted her up
and gave her a beautiful new name—
"DEPENDENCE!"
The next day Dependence came face to face
with the handsome young man in the office.
Where have you been? he asked.
Someone said you died, but you look pretty
good to me—good enough to eat, in fact!
Then. . . . Tonight? he whispered in her ear.

Not tonight, not tomorrow—never again!
Dependence answered quietly.
She was very nervous and looked around for Jesus.
He was there, of course,
standing in the shadows—
smiling.

THEN THE BIRDS SANG!

WORKSHEET

Chapter 5

I. OUR ADVERSARY: Read Job 1:6–12 and 2.
   a. What do we learn about God from this passage?
   b. What do we learn about Satan?

II. OUR ADVOCATE: Read Hebrews 8:1–13.
   a. Make a list of the things in this passage that awe you.
   b. Make a list of the things that comfort you.
   c. Make a list of the things that challenge you.

III. OUR ANSWER: Think of a failure in your life. Which verse or thought from today's lesson can be your answer?

IV. PRAYERTIME: Read Ephesians 6:10–17.
   a. Praise God for the armor He has provided to protect you from Satan.
   b. Praise God for providing Jesus to be your advocate.
   c. Pray for people who are discouraged by failures.

Chapter 6

FIRE

Acts 2:1–4

When the day of Pentecost came, they were all together in one place. Suddenly a sound like the blowing of a violent wind came from heaven and filled the whole house where they were sitting. They saw what seemed to be tongues of fire that separated and came to rest on each of them. All of them were filled with the Holy Spirit and began to speak in other tongues as the Spirit enabled them.

Acts 2:1–4

A Promise of Power

Can't you imagine Peter asking the Lord after their breakfast by the sea, "How can I be sure I won't fail You again? Where will I find the power to find the sheep and shepherd the lambs?"

And can't you almost hear Jesus' reply to His inquisitive apostle, which was in effect, "Wait, and the power will be given to you"?

The disciples were told this after Jesus' death and resurrection, while His followers were still trying to grasp the miracle that He was alive. He explained to them some things about His kingdom and the role they were to play in it. And then He told them, "Stay in the city until you have been clothed with power from on high" (Luke 24:49).

Now, that must have sounded like good news to Peter and the others. Power was just what they needed! And the Lord Jesus promised that empowerment would come soon: "In a few days you will be baptized with the Holy Spirit" (Acts 1:5).

The disciples were reminded of this promise of power right after Jesus ascended into heaven. Two angels appeared and told the watching disciples to stop gazing up into the sky, because "this same Jesus, who has been taken from you into heaven, will come back in the same way you have seen him go into heaven" (Acts 1:11). In the meantime, the angel implied, there were things to do!

So the disciples obeyed the angel's injunction and the Lord's command. They waited in Jerusalem, busying themselves with prayer until they were empowered for their ministry.

The disciples were gathered together to celebrate the Jewish Feast of Pentecost when it happened. The sounds of heaven announced the Spirit's grand arrival, and all the people in Jerusalem were drawn to the vicinity to see what all the commotion was about.

The Spirit touched each man and woman gathered together in turn, igniting them all with the flame of God's love and power. And then they tumbled out of their meeting place into the streets of the city, sharing the gospel in languages they had never even learned.

This miracle, witnessed by hundreds of people of all tongues and nations who were gathered from all corners of the Roman empire for the feast, gave Peter a golden opportunity. Standing up unashamed and unafraid, endued with power from heaven, he preached a powerful message which resulted in three thousand people committing their lives to Christ Jesus.

Not bad for a day's work! And what a fulfillment to Jesus' promise of power!

A New Meaning for Pentecost

When the Spirit was poured out at Pentecost, God imparted to many what had previously been the privilege of the few. In days gone by, there had been a selective outpouring, but now each of the Lord's followers was endued with the power of the Holy Spirit. What is more, the gift of the Spirit was given permanently, whereas before the Spirit had only been available temporarily. For Jesus had promised His disciples, "And surely I will be with you always, to the very end of the age" (Matt. 28:20).

It is deeply significant to me that all this happened during the Jewish celebration of Pentecost—or the Feast of Weeks. This holiday was celebrated fifty days (seven weeks) after the Feast of Unleavened Bread, a ceremony in which a sheaf of grain—the "first fruits" of the barley harvest—was waved before the Lord (see Lev. 23:15). The sheaf of grain was offered right after Passover, during the first month of the Jewish year. Then at Pentecost, seven weeks later, another kind of "first fruit" was offered to the Lord—loaves of bread risen and alive with leaven, which were prepared from the harvested wheat.

These practices can take on a beautiful new meaning in light of the New Testament events. For it is no coincidence that Jesus died at Passover, rose again about the time the sheaf of grain was offered, and then, fifty days later at Pentecost, sent the promised Holy Spirit to make His church one and set it aflame with His power!

The picture in the New Testament struck me as one which is very beautiful. Instead of presenting to the Lord individual growths of grain, loosely bound together, there was to be a weaving and union of the particles, blending the grain into one, homogeneous body—in fact, one loaf.

In 1 Corinthians 10:16–17, Paul uses this very picture: "Is not the cup of thanksgiving for which we all give thanks a participation in the blood of Christ? And is not the bread that we break a participation in the body of Christ? Because there is one loaf, we, who are many, are one body, for we all partake of the one loaf."

The Forever Family

Pentecost, then, resulted in a common binding together of God's forever family. Before His death and resurrection, Jesus Himself had been the unifying factor, but this had been limiting because the Lord had been confined to His earthly body. Now the indwelling Spirit, given without measure, was to bring together all those who believed in Him.

Once, while I was waiting for a flight at a Washington airport, my attention was drawn to a group of excited couples. All of them had strollers with them, and baby paraphernalia was all over the place, but there were no babies in sight. I discovered these eight couples had never met before that particular moment, and I watched them curiously as they made polite but restrained conversation.

Suddenly the plane they were waiting for arrived, and into the eager waiting arms of these couples were placed eight beautiful Korean orphans, all about three months old. What a transformation took place among those excited people—they suddenly became almost like one big family. Those of us watching from outside their experience laughed and cried with them at this marvelous gift of new life, but none of us could identify with them the way they suddenly seemed to identify with each other.

After all, these new parents had something very unique in common. They laughed—and cried a little, too—as they began to show off their babies to each other. They chattered happily together as if they had known each other all their lives. They didn't seem to be able to tear themselves away, even though relatives and friends were waiting impatiently to whisk them off to home and celebration.

That same sort of "binding" quality comes about among human beings who stretch out their spiritual arms and accept God's gift of new life into their hearts. After I became a Christian, I couldn't get over this "family" feeling. I felt it whenever I met a bunch of believers. Even though we often had very little in common apart from our faith in Christ, I somehow felt we had known each other a very long time.

This sense of family crossed all barriers, so that the "oneness" operated even when I was introduced to a total stranger. This was really wonderful because I felt a true sense of belonging. I'd come home to the family of God. And today, years later, I still rejoice in being one of the family!

A Launching and Equipping Power

The giving of the Holy Spirit at Pentecost also launched spiritually what had only been understood politically. The everlasting kingdom was to go far beyond the political realm. It was to be an eternal spiritual experience that would be entered into on earth, yet enjoyed in all of its fullness and consummation in heaven. Pentecost saw the founding of the worldwide church of Jesus Christ.

And then there was a practical aspect to what happened at Pentecost. Once it had brought the people of God together, the Holy Spirit at Pentecost equipped them to do the work of ministry.

How could Peter possibly tend the Lord's flock without God's giving him the ability to be a good sheep and a good shepherd all at the same time? That would necessitate a good Spirit's giving him the good power to be goodly—or godly. That is what Peter received at Pentecost. And that is what

Pentecost promises all of us—a thorough equipping where previously we have known only inadequate strength.

I tried so hard to quit swearing when I first became a Christian. No one else seemed to swear quite so easily as I did—or with such relish! I realized that change was absolutely necessary if I was to lead others to a Christ who was supposed to make a difference; a dirty mouth is no mouth for telling the gospel story! But try though I might, I couldn't stop those naughty words from slipping out on the slightest provocation.

The Holy Spirit who had come into my life, however, was obviously horrified at such an unruly tongue and lost no time inwardly "checking" me every time I was about to let rip! And then, once my tongue was curbed, I discovered a teaching gift that went far beyond the classroom walls.

As I taught children math and English, they learned math and English. But as I taught them about the Lord, they caught my love for Him and gave their lives over to the Holy Spirit, who began to make the same differences in their lives as He had in mine. I discovered that God had equipped me with an effective gift of teaching spiritual truths.

Who Is the Holy Spirit?

The Holy Spirit, moving at Pentecost, bound together and empowered the followers of Christ to be His people in the world. And the Holy Spirit does the same for us today. But just who *is* this third Person of the Trinity?

When Jesus spoke about the Holy Spirit to His disciples, they knew what He was talking about. The idea of the Holy Spirit was not a strange one to them—although the dramatic outpouring at Pentecost must have been a surprise! Being steeped in the Old Testament, the disciples knew Joel's prophecy well. Hadn't God said through the prophet, "I will pour out my Spirit on all people. Your sons and daughters will prophesy, your old men will dream dreams, your young men will see visions. Even on my servants, both men and women, I will pour out my Spirit in those days" (Joel 2:28–29).

For those of us, however, who do not have a Jewish background, the whole concept of the Holy Spirit is much more difficult to understand. I grew up attending a traditional English school, and I heard about the "Holy Ghost" regularly. Every day during school prayers—compulsory in England—we would recite the Anglican Creed, and I along with all my little friends would pipe up at the appropriate time, "I believe in the Holy Ghost."

Sometimes, as my childish mind wandered around the words, I would wonder who the Holy Ghost was. Was He a sheet-shrouded spook who haunted old English churchyards? A ghost had a rather frightening connotation to a small child.

Power That Makes a Difference

Small children aren't the only ones who have misunderstandings about the third member of the Trinity. Some talk of Him as an "it," and others treat Him almost as if He's a toy to play with. For one He is merely a subject for conferences, while for another He is a vague "influence."

The Scriptures, however, tell us some very specific things about who the Holy Spirit is and what He does. But before we try to see what the Scripture says about the Holy Spirit, we need to realize one important fact: He makes a difference!

Corporately, His coming at Pentecost made the difference in transforming a loose collection of followers into a unified body of believers. And Pentecost made the difference in individuals as well. For example, the Spirit took a Simon and turned him permanently and forever into a Peter!

Before Pentecost, Peter ran away from a little servant girl who challenged his allegiance to Christ. After Pentecost, he stood up in front of thousands of people—among whom were the killers of Jesus—and preached such a powerful message that three thousand were converted.

Oh yes, the Holy Spirit makes a difference! But then Jesus had already promised the disciples that He would!

The Lord had taught that there was a distinction between the Father and Himself, and that there was another person called "the Counselor" whom the Father would send in His name (John 14:26) and who would be with them forever (John 14:16). Jesus explained that He had to go away so that this "Helper" could come, and that this would be far better for them once His work was finished and the Holy Spirit's was begun.

Divine Abilities

The Holy Spirit, you see, is a divine Person with divine abilities. If the Holy Spirit is indeed a coequal member of the Trinity, it stands to reason that He's going to make changes when He enters our lives.

First of all, the Holy Spirit will help us to know what we need to know about Him. That's because He is omniscient and therefore He obviously knows all there is to know about Himself. He promises to let us in on the secret. Paul says, "For who could really understand a man's inmost thoughts except the spirit of the man himself? How much less could anyone understand the thoughts of God except the very Spirit of God?" (1 Cor. 2:11, PHILLIPS). When we cry out in prayer to know if God is really there—and, if He is there, what He is like and, more important, what He wants us to do with the knowledge of His "thereness" and "likeness"—then the Holy Spirit will explain it all to us. He is an excellent teacher who will lead us into all truth (John 16:13).

The Holy Spirit is not only divinely all-knowing or omniscient; He is also omnipresent—capable of being everywhere at once. This knowledge was a significant source of comfort to me after Stuart and I accepted an invitation to leave England and live in the United States. I had struggled for words to tell my widowed mother we were leaving. And as I expected, she was devastated by the news. She had not traveled much, and the thought of our going so far away was a crushing blow to her. She could never see herself traveling across the sea, and so she really believed she would never see her grandchildren again. "I think it's having the ocean between us that is making me feel you will be so far away," she explained sadly.

I, too, felt a great sorrow about our separation, and I turned to the Psalms for comfort. Reading Psalm 139, I came across the words, "Where can I go from your Spirit? Where can I flee from your presence? If I go up to the heavens, you are there; if I make my bed in the depths, you are there. If I rise on the wings of the dawn, if I settle on the far side of the sea, even there your hand will guide me, your right hand will hold me fast" (vv. 7–10). Sharing these words together, my mother and I promised to pray for each other. And we found comfort in the fact that if the same Holy Spirit who indwelt us both was not fazed by distance, then we needn't be, either! I'm sure Peter learned to thank God for the Holy Spirit's ever-presentness when he, too, began to move out to the far corners of the world for Christ—far from blue Galilee and all those he loved.

The Holy Spirit is omnipotent, too. That means He is all-powerful. This aspect of the Godhead was the needed element in Peter's experience. He needed God's power for his immediate circumstances and his ongoing ministry. And we need that power, too.

Whenever God Does Anything Big

I once heard my husband make a statement I have never forgotten: "Whenever God does anything big, He does it by His Spirit." Then Stuart went on to say that creation, incarnation, crucifixion, resurrection, and regeneration are all the Spirit's work—as is gifting for evangelization.

Is the church powerless today? Maybe that is because we are trying to shake the world without the World Shaker—the Holy Spirit. Could it be that we have been inadequately instructed in the doctrine of the Holy Ghost?

It took power to turn a shivering, cowardly Simon into a powerful, preaching Peter—more power than the big fisherman could ever manufacture himself. When you come across a verse such as "And if the Spirit of him who raised Jesus from the dead is living in you, he who raised Christ from the dead will also give life to your mortal bodies through his Spirit, who lives in you" (Rom. 8:11), then the impossible task of preaching to lost sheep and convincing them they are lost, then feeding "found ones" and persuading them to follow along becomes a gloriously possible privilege!

The trouble is that all too often we keep trying to do the Spirit's work for Him. The Bible says it is the Spirit's work—not ours—to approach someone's soul and to convict and convince that person of sin!

Have you ever tried to tell someone who is without belief or one who already is a pretty "religious" person that he or she is a sinner? If you have done it in your own strength, you most probably got your head knocked off. Before Pentecost, Peter didn't even try convincing the temple guards or Pharisees of their need. But many of these same men came to Peter's first church service and were soundly converted!

John 16:8 tells us it is the Spirit's work to convert people. It is true that He often chooses to make our earthly bodies vehicles of His divine action and uses us to do His work—but He can work apart from us as well. And we all need to come to grips with the fact that we can't convert, convict, or convince anybody of anything spiritual without first being convicted, converted, and convinced ourselves! Then it becomes a matter of letting Him loose through our personalities. As Peter says, "If anyone speaks, he should do it as one speaking the very words of God. If anyone serves, he should do it with the strength God provides, so that in all things God may be praised through Jesus Christ. To him be the glory and the power for ever and ever. Amen" (1 Pet. 4:11).

How the Spirit Works in Us

The Holy Spirit abides in us to do many things to, for, and through us. First of all, He confirms the truth as it is in Jesus to our hearts so we can go out and about and confirm it to others.

Have you ever harbored the nagging doubt that you may have made a terrible mistake when you became a Christian? I must admit that I have on a few occasions wondered if I was really right and so many other people were really wrong! I mean, isn't it the height of arrogance to believe you have found *the* truth and not just *a* truth? Many a college friend challenged me on such an assumption.

"How come you think God is someone special to you and you are special to Him?" my best friend asked me in a somewhat hostile manner shortly after my conversion. It did all sound sort of proud, and I worried.

Then, however, I read the Bible, "The Spirit himself testifies with our spirit that we are God's children. Now if we are children, then we are heirs—heirs of God and co-heirs with Christ" (Rom. 8:16–17). And through this verse I realized that it was the Holy Spirit who whispered His Father's assurances to my spirit. He confirmed the fact that Jesus claimed not to be merely another voice in a world full of voices, but *the voice* of all voices; not a way, but *the way;* not a truth, but *the truth;* not a life, but *the life* (John 16:6)!

Peter had to answer his contemporaries on this very issue. How was it, they asked, that the religion that his fathers died for wasn't good enough for him? And how dare he tell them it wasn't good enough for them, either? What was this newfangled doctrine about this Jesus of Nazareth? Had he stopped believing in the Messiah? In answer, Peter climaxed his wonderful sermon of Pentecost with these words: "Therefore let all Israel be assured of this: God has made this Jesus, whom you crucified, both Lord and Christ" (Acts 2:36).

It is hard to face people with the possibility that religious truths they have sincerely held all their lives may be wrong—or perhaps just part of the truth. It is possible, you know, to be sincere and yet be sincerely wrong! But it is going to take the work of the Holy Spirit to convict and convert people of that, and He will not do so if that truth is not confirmed within our own hearts first.

Look what happened to the listeners on that day of Pentecost: "When the people heard this [Peter's sermon], they were cut to the heart and said to Peter and the other apostles, 'Brothers, what shall we do?' Peter replied, 'Repent and be baptized, every one of you, in the name of Jesus Christ so that your sins may be forgiven. And you will receive the gift of the Holy Spirit'" (Acts 2:37–38).

Not only does the indwelling Holy Spirit do His convicting and convincing work through us; He also comforts us when we are weak or worried and helps us with our doubts and fears. I have experienced great joy on nights when God has used me to speak at a meeting and many people have become Christians as a result. On those very same nights, however, I have experienced great fear as I have been alone in a strange place or been worried about one of our children far away. When that happened, the same Holy Spirit who gave me help to help others gave me help to help myself! He is indeed the Comforter!

And then He also conforms us to the image of Christ. It is not just going to be a matter of the words we speak that will do the job, but the sense of the Spirit about our lives. His likeness formed in us should be an attractive presence alerting people to the fact of our delight about our indwelling guest! This should then cause some to comment or others to respond to our words.

Now, I am not talking about outward labels, here. Once I was at a women's gathering where no one was aware I was a pastor's wife. It was wonderful; no one worried about her language or treated me like a religious pariah! Then someone unfortunately recognized me and introduced me—not as Jill, but as "the pastor's wife"! And things suddenly changed. All at once, people began apologizing for their bad language and telling me nervously how they just loved to go to church, especially at Easter or Christmas. Their friends assured me they helped in the March of Dimes. I found that the tag, "pastor's wife" was a real barrier to normal conversation and that it created the strangest reactions to me as a person. People responded to me according to their preconceived notions of what the pastor's wife was probably like!

I want to be a spirit-filled Christian, and not just someone with a religious job description, a tag that frightens people away. I think of another, much different occasion, when a new friend initiated a conversation with me by saying shyly, "There's something about you, Jill, that I can't quite put my finger on! It's a sort of 'power,' yet gentle and sweet!" My heart laughed with joy, and I hastened to tell her it must be Jesus she sensed, as I was neither gentle nor sweet!

Beatrice Cleland's beautiful poem "Indwelt" (from *Thank You for Being a Friend*) sums it up for me:

Not only by the words you say, not only in your deeds
    confessed,
  But in the most unconscious way is Christ expressed.
  Is it a beatific smile, a holy light upon your brow?
  Oh no! I felt His presence when you laughed just now.
For me, t'was not the truth you taught . . . to you so clear, to
    me so dim,
  But when you came to me, you brought a sense of Him.
And from your eyes He beckons me and from your lips His
    love is shed,
  'Til I lose sight of you and see the Christ instead.

That is exactly what I pray the Holy Spirit will work in and through me! The Holy Spirit's abiding presence alerts folk to His person, not our person!

Anointed for His Service

Not only does the Holy Spirit abide in us to do all this wonderful work; He also anoints us for His service, commanding us to witness for Him.

So where do we start? In Jerusalem!

Peter had already received the command to witness before he ever received the power to do it—and that command was very specific about *where* to witness first. Hadn't the Lord Jesus told all of the disciples that they would be witnesses unto Him starting in Jerusalem, *then* in Samaria, and then to the uttermost parts of the earth (Acts 1:8)?

But Peter would need an awful lot of help to start in Jerusalem! That was the place of his biggest failure, the place he had denied the Lord, and therefore the most difficult place of all.

So often, when we have made a terrible mistake, we find ourselves wanting to "start over" somewhere else. Instead, we need to go back to the place of failure and face things right there. "Jerusalem first" can mean our hometown, or our closest relative, or our dearest friend or colleague. It is always the most difficult commission to witness to the people who know us best—the reason being that it matters so much!

Imagine a husband who finds the Lord Jesus Christ as his Savior. His Jerusalem becomes his wife, who hasn't found the Lord. Or think of friends who play racquetball together. One of them finds faith, and his Jerusalem becomes the other who hasn't. Or what about a teenage girl, the youngest in a big family, who comes home after a youth meeting with Jesus in her heart, a spring in her step, and a great anxiety about the reception she is going to receive! Her Jerusalem is her living room and her rather liberal-living mom and dad—to say nothing of her more liberal-living sisters, brothers, and friends!

To share Christ in Jerusalem is certainly not an easy thing to do. It wasn't easy for Peter, but he did it, because it was a command from the Lord. But even though Peter was filled with the Holy Spirit in the Upper Room, he still had a choice to make. He had to walk out into the streets of Jerusalem and obey that command to be a witness. The Holy Spirit does not carry us around against our will on some sort of unseen spiritual wings; He calls us to be witnesses in our Jerusalem and to use our own two feet to take us to do it. Then, as we obey, He comes alongside to lend us His aid.

Commissioned to Care

We are also commissioned to care as we witness. It doesn't work to preach without passion or to lecture without love. And this, too, is the work of the Holy Spirit.

When Peter had finished his first great sermon on the day of Pentecost, the Scriptures say he moved among the people and "pleaded with them, 'Save yourselves from this corrupt generation'" (Acts 2:40). He didn't just preach—he passionately pleaded.

But where did Peter get this kind of loving concern? When Jesus and Peter had walked together by the Sea of Galilee after Jesus' resurrection, Peter had had to face the fact that his love was limited. Remember, when Jesus asked Peter, "Do you love me?", He had used the strongest Greek word for love He could find—*agape,* or unconditional love. And Peter had had to answer using the lesser Greek word for love: "No Lord—I'm only 'fond of you.'"

But after Peter made this shamefaced admission about the limits of his love, Jesus simply replied, "Feed my sheep." He was saying, in effect, "Let's start with what you've got. Give me the little love you do have, Peter, and my Spirit will grow it into a bigger love!"

I believe that's what the Lord says to us when He commissions us to care. If we wait until our hearts "ache" for people before we act lovingly or witness to them, we will wait forever. But if we move ahead as we are told, the love ache "grows as we goes"—as someone has aptly said.

It worked for Peter! For when we read his later letters to his flock, we find ourselves reading love letters. Peter had been commissioned to care. But he learned that caring takes obedience and action, which involves us in time with real people in real situations. As we act in caring concern, the Holy Spirit grows agape love in the seedbeds of our hearts.

As the brand-new Christian community settled down in Jerusalem to care for each other, they found plenty of opportunities to practice practical caring and love. We read, "All the believers were together and had everything in common. Selling their possessions and goods, they gave to anyone as he had need" (Acts 2:44–45). This undoubtedly included Peter and his wife and all the other disciples and their families.

And this is exactly where the rubber meets the road for us! To give a bag of clothes to Goodwill—especially when we want them out of the way anyway—or even to take items of groceries to church for the food pantry—usually things no one will eat at home because no one particularly likes them—is *not* what these verses are talking about. These early Christians cared enough to take precious possessions and share them with some who had nothing else in the whole world. Land, houses, jewelry, cattle, and business interests were all taken and laid at the apostles' feet. It takes the work of the Holy Spirit in our lives to pry our grubby little grasping fingers off "our" possessions so that others may possess them instead.

Bible Pictures

The Holy Spirit, if I may put it reverently, is an extremely busy Person! He does so many things in so many places and in so many ways! To help us grasp the breadth of His work, the Bible uses several pictures to help us.

When a Jewish leader called Nicodemus came to Jesus by night to inquire about God, Jesus looked straight at him and told him he had to be born again. Nicodemus couldn't understand this concept, and Jesus used a picture to help him "see" the truth. He explained that it was the Holy Spirit's work to bring spiritual life to a man's soul, and He likened the Spirit to a wind that blows where it wills. He explained that we don't know where the wind comes from and we don't know where it goes; we only see the effect it has! We cannot understand the Holy Spirit, either, but we can experience the gift of His changing work in our lives (John 3:1–21).

Jesus used another picture to explain the Holy Spirit's work—water. As He journeyed through Samaria, He was tired, so He rested by a well. His disciples went away to buy bread, and a woman of doubtful reputation came to draw water. The Lord, knowing the thirst of her soul, told her that, if she asked Him, He would give her "living water" so that she would never thirst again (John 4:1–26).

The Lord Jesus used this symbol of water another time to great effect. On the last and greatest day of the Feast of the Tabernacles, when water was used as a symbol of God's provision for the children of Israel in the desert, Jesus stood up at an appropriate moment in the proceedings and cried out in a loud voice, "If a man is thirsty, let him come to me and drink. Whoever believes in me, as the Scripture has said, streams of living water will flow from within him." The gospel writer adds, "By this he meant the Spirit, whom those who believed in him were later to receive. Up to that time the Spirit had not been given, since Jesus had not yet been glorified" (John 7:37–39).

The Bible gives other pictures of the Spirit to help us grasp something of His person and work. He is spoken of as a dove (Matt. 3:16), a seal (Eph. 1:13, 4:30), and oil (Heb. 1:9). All these pictures are rich in meaning.

A dove symbolizes self-sacrifice, for this sweet, gentle bird, it is said, always offered its neck to the knife. In the temple, living sacrifices were brought to the priests, and the dove's behavior was in stark contrast to the behavior of other animals, who would make a lot of noise as they went to their deaths. The Holy Spirit enables us to live sacrificially, without making a lot of noise about it!

A seal, or pledge, was a picture that could have many meanings to the people of Bible times. The Holy Spirit is spoken of as God's pledge of future happiness (Eph. 1:13–14). In those days, at a betrothal—vaguely equivalent to our engagement—pledges would be given and taken concerning the promises made to be ratified later at the marriage ceremony. If you like, we can take that lovely picture and apply it to our culture, saying that the Holy Spirit is like God's engagement ring given to a loved one as a pledge of future blessedness—a future blessedness to be ratified at the marriage supper of the Lamb. A seal also speaks of ownership, security, authenticity, and authority. Any or all of these pictures are heavy with meaning.

Oil is one of the symbols most frequently used to speak of the Holy Spirit. Oil was used to anoint the prophet, the priest, and the king to set them apart for a speaking, listening, or reigning ministry! What a great picture for small people who have come to know such a great God—a God who commands us to be His prophets witnessing to His truth, who commissions us to care and to listen as the good priest listens with love and tender compassion to those in trouble, and who calls us to reign as kings in life with Christ Jesus. The Holy Spirit wants to make all of this and more available to us in rich spiritual resource.

Responding to the Spirit

So if these are but a few of the wonderful things the Holy Spirit does for us, our hearts should respond. We should ask, What are some of the things we can do for Him?

First of all, we can yield to Him. How do we do this? We ask in prayer for His help to obey Him as Lord. To begin to be sensitive to the Spirit's voice will require time set aside in order to listen to what He is saying. No man calls Jesus Lord but by the Spirit. So we must know we cannot even live for the Lord without His help.

To be controlled by the Spirit, we will need to be "filled with the Spirit," as Ephesians commands us to be. We need to tell Him we'll do whatever He wants us to do; then we can ask Him to make those "doings" clear through His Word—or through other Christians, circumstances, inner convictions, common sense, or all of these things put together.

The opposite of yielding is resisting or fighting. There is no middle ground. We are told specifically not to resist the Spirit or His truth (James 4:7). As the Holy Spirit explains God's truth to us and then enables us to obey it by providing the power, He expects us in return to be truthful in our response. He is the Spirit of Truth, so lies grieve Him deeply.

Remember that the Holy Spirit is a Person, so it follows we can treat Him as a Person. We can respect and love and obey His promptings, or we can resist and grieve Him. *Grieve* is a love word! We can only really grieve someone who loves us. And Ephesians 4:30–31 tells us in no uncertain terms, "Do not grieve the Holy Spirit of God, with which you were sealed for the day of redemption."

A good example of grieving the Holy Spirit is the bad example of Ananias and Sapphira, whose story is told in Acts 5. In the early days of the Jerusalem church, all the believers were living together in community, sharing everything. When someone in the fellowship had a need, another who was more fortunate met it. Barnabas was a wealthy man who owned land on the island of Cyprus. He sold it and brought the money, laying it at the apostles' feet. Ananias and Sapphira watched the man's actions with a grudging respect and admiration. They had land, too. They wanted to look good in the people's eyes, like Barnabas. They coveted the way people admired the generous man. But they couldn't quite bring themselves to do what he had done, so they thought out a plan. They would sell the land and give half of the purchase price to the church, keeping the other half for themselves.

Now, there was absolutely nothing wrong with that; actually, it was an extremely generous thing to do. But the plan didn't stop there. Ananias and Sapphira decided to tell a lie! They would pretend they had given all the money they received for the land, when in reality they would be withholding some of it. Now, as Peter pointed out to them, that was definitely a lie—a big black one, and a lie not to men, but to the Holy Ghost Himself.

When faced with their deception, Ananias and Sapphira both fell down and died, and great fear came upon everybody. I bet it did! Whenever I hear about people wanting to go back to the early days of Christianity, I think of this incident and shudder. How many funerals would we have in a week? How many times do I say, "Lord, You have my time" and He answers, "You're a liar!" Or "Lord, You have my love," yet my heart is divided in its loyalties?

How glad I am that I am not living in Jerusalem in those days! Yet Ananias and Sapphira's sin is as grievious today as then, and it takes its own destructive toll inside us. Whenever we tell a lie to the Holy Spirit, something dies in our own spirits. If we continually grieve the Spirit, we are effectively killing the love relationship between us.

Thinking about this, I penned the following words:

The Hypocrite

Here I am on my knees—how nice.
I hope the church is watching—
  especially Mrs. Rice.
I hope You're impressed, Lord,
  with my attitude of prayer.

Did I hear a little voice say,
I'm not even there!
You don't need me or want me;
You're praying lost in sin?
Not so, Lord, cries indignant me
Just You listen in!
All my prayers are beautiful—
just ask Mrs. Prior.
I've given You my prayer life, Lord—
He answered: *You're a liar!*

Here I am, it's offering time—how nice.
I'll rattle the coins so they'll all hear—
especially Mrs. Rice.
What's that I've kept inside my purse?
Ha! That's not for You, You know.
I know You'll understand.
The cost of living's gone up so,
And I'm saving up for holidays—
a tour is my desire.
You *know* You own my money,
Lord!
He whispered: *You're a liar.*

Here I am, its altar call—how nice.
Now's my chance to show the way—
especially to Mrs. Rice.
Well! Mrs. Rice is coming too—
the hypocrite—she's crying!
I can't believe that's genuine;
God will condemn—she's lying!
Now I've come here to give my life,
no honor could be higher!
You know You have my everything. . . .
He thundered: *YOU'RE A LIAR!*

So what can I do for the Holy Spirit when He does so much for me? I can yield and not resist Him, love and not grieve Him. And I can stir up the fire within and not quench Him!

Stirring Up the Fire

The picture we started with in the Upper Room is the one we can finish with. On the day of Pentecost, something like a tongue of fire appeared over each one of the disciples' heads. Fire is a symbol of energy, of warmth, of an all-consuming power. We are to stir up that fire by whatever means it takes to keep the flame bright. Whether it be to "stoke" the flames with Bible reading, prayers, worship, or witness or to guard it from the "cold water" many would throw upon it, the fire must be kept burning brightly in an increasingly dark and hostile world.

"Do not put out the Spirit's fire," says Paul in 1 Thessalonians 5:19—or, in another translation, "Quench not the Spirit" (KJV).

We can quench the fire of the Spirit by simply smothering the fire with blankets of trivia, or by dumping the sands of cynicism or the waters of worry all over Him. On the other hand, we can tend the fires of the Spirit so that they never go out and the work of God is worked out through us in our own generation. Peter, endued and empowered by the Spirit, learned to stir up the gift within him as he grew to love and not grieve his heavenly Guest. May we learn to do that, too!

WORKSHEET

Chapter 6

I. Review what you learned about the following symbols used in Scripture to describe the Holy Spirit. Which symbol meant most to you and why?

OIL—Hebrews 1:9
WATER—John 7:38–39
WIND—John 3:8, Acts 2:2
FIRE—Acts 2:3
DOVE—Matthew 3:16
SEAL—Ephesians 1:13, 4:30

II. Read Peter's sermon at Pentecost recorded in Acts 2:14–36.

a. Which specific verse shows you that the Holy Spirit had changed Peter?

b. Why did you choose the particular verse you did? (If you are meeting in a group, there will be several different verses chosen. Discuss your reasons for choosing.)

III. PRAYERTIME: Read Acts 5:1–11. Pray about the lessons learned from this passage.

a. If you haven't already, perhaps you would like to pray a prayer inviting the Holy Spirit to come into your life. You may want to "borrow" these words: *"Lord Jesus, by Your grace forgive my many sins. Thank You for dying for me to make forgiveness possible. Now, by Your Holy Spirit, come into my heart and be my Savior. Empower me to be Your witness, encourage me when I am down, enlighten me as I read Your Word, and enrich me beyond my wildest dreams. Amen."*

b. Take a moment to thank Him for the meaning He has brought into your life, just as He promised He would.

Chapter 7

CRUTCHES

Acts 3:1–8

One day Peter and John were going up to the temple at the time of prayer—at three in the afternoon. Now a man crippled from birth was being carried to the temple gate called Beautiful, where he was put every day to beg from those going into the temple courts. When he saw Peter and John about to enter, he asked them for money. Peter looked straight at him, as did John. Then Peter said, "Look at us!" So the man gave them his attention, expecting to get something from them. Then Peter said, "Silver or gold I do not have, but what I have I give you. In the name of Jesus Christ of Nazareth, walk." Taking him by the right hand, he helped him up, and instantly the man's feet and ankles became strong. He jumped to his feet and began to walk. Then he went with them into the temple courts, walking and jumping, and praising God.

Acts 3:1–8

Crippled, Carried, and Crying

Peter and John went up to the temple to pray. At the entrance, there was a man on a mat who had been crippled from birth. Something was terribly wrong with him, and this problem prevented his walking tall and straight before God and other people.

This man's problem was physical. But there are other kinds of problems that are just as crippling. For something is terribly wrong with our world, just as something was wrong with the crippled man by the temple gate. Think of all the crippled marriages and the emotionally crippled kids that come from them. The news daily informs us of the scourge of AIDS and warns us that some nut may be contaminating our store-bought goods with cyanide. Babies are being born already addicted to cocaine and heroin.

What is wrong with us? As God scans mankind's horizons, He sees a world full of spiritually handicapped people. For sin has crippled mankind, and we are all affected one way or another.

So at the gate Beautiful lay this cruelly crippled man—crooked from birth. He represents our sinful shape. For the Bible tells us our mothers conceived us in sin and that is our problem (Ps. 51:5).

What does this mean? In my hometown in the British Isles, there is a beautiful little park where elderly men and women, bent by age, sport straw hats and pass the time of day playing the game of bowls. The game is not to be confused with tenpin bowling; it is another game altogether. At first glance, it seems a very simple matter to roll the big black ball toward the little white one, which is called a jack. The object of the exercise is to try and get the big ball as near the little one as possible without actually hitting it. Now this appears to be suitable pastime for old people—rather like a grownup's game of marbles, but it's a lot harder than it looks. For inside each black ball is a weight that is set off-center.

Thus the internal bias tends to pull the ball away from the target.

Watching the old people play their game conjured up for me a vivid picture of sin in the heart of humankind. No matter how directly people are aimed toward the target of rightness, an internal bias pulls them off-center. Isn't it true that we aim our children toward "goodness" but so many times see them peel off to the left or right before ever arriving at the goal we set for them? Whoever taught our kids to disobey us, to answer back, to tell lies? Somehow they knew how to do all that quite naturally!

Paul called this principle inside us the "old nature," or the sin principle. It is that element in us which wants its own way, and it will only be fixed when Christ's new nature is imparted to us by the Holy Spirit. He can strengthen us and help us to control the old nature and correct our direction. He will enable us to hit the jack.

Man was not originally created with a propensity to sin, but free will gave him the opportunity. And when sin first entered the human race through Adam, his sinful nature was passed on to all of humanity—including you and me. It is not hard to believe that all humankind is hobbled or crippled by its own selfish whims and caprices.

Not only was the man at the temple gate crippled; he was dependent as well. He had been carried to his place of "work" that particular day perhaps by friends or family, and he was daily dependent upon others to carry him anywhere he wanted to go.

Thousands upon thousands of us are dependent on others for all sorts of things—not least our livelihoods. In fact, for many dependence can become a life or death situation. Some people are financially dependent. Perhaps a young wife has been left by her husband and has been unable to procure child support. Or maybe an old man has given all his welfare checks to his children, who "look in on him" once in a while (*once* being the operative word).

Not only are many people financially dependent, but many are physically dependent, too. It's demeaning and degrading to have strangers wash and handle you, and yet to have loved ones do it can cause even worse misery and embarrassment. Sickness and old age can be very cruel. Having taught our children to practice self-indulgence in their youth, we reap the consequences in our twilight years.

And what about the psychologically dependent? There are plenty of emotionally hobbled people around who are thoroughly controlled by a close friend or a closer relative. These are the folk who fall apart if their child goes to school angry at them. People can be dominated by other people to the point that they just don't seem to be able to live free from trying to "perform" to please or "produce" to be accepted.

This is a crying shame. For not only is our world crippled by sin and carried by circumstances, it is crying out for help—like the crippled man at the gate Beautiful who, seeing Peter and John about to enter, asked them for money (Acts 3:3). Our world is begging for attention. How many people sitting outside the gates of our beautiful churches are watching the believers coming and going to their religious meetings? Outside looking in, they wonder what on earth Christianity is all about. They have a crying need, even though most do not even know what they are crying about.

I think of teenagers particularly. So often their wild makeup or hairstyles are a plea for attention. And if these kids aren't crying for attention by the way they dress, they may be doing so by their behavior or eating habits.

Look at Us!

One thing is certain, the man at the temple gate was used to the disinterest of the worshipers and was not expecting too much from Peter and John. He certainly got the shock of his life! Peter, fastening his eyes on him, said, "Look at us!" (v. 4). So the man gave them his attention. Two seconds later, he was on his feet for the very first time in his life!

When Christians witness to the Lord Jesus, in effect they are saying, "Look at us! We have something to give you." Maybe crippled people don't expect very much, but we can always surprise them. The greatest thing we can ever give a spiritually disabled man is not a crutch or even a handout, but a word from God that will stand him up on his own two feet and set him off on the right road.

"Then Peter said to the man, 'Silver or gold I do not have, but what I have I give you. In the name of Jesus Christ of Nazareth, walk.' Taking him by the right hand, he helped him up, and instantly the man's feet and ankles became strong. He jumped to his feet and began to walk. Then he went with them into the temple courts, walking and jumping, and praising God" (Acts 3:6–8).

We, like Peter and John, must tell a hurting world to look to us so we can point them to Him. We can witness to the fact that we were once crippled, too, until Jesus walked by and took us by the hand and told us to get up and walk. It is in His name and power, not our own, that we can do this and so can they.

Not long ago, I was leading a series of meetings in one of the western states. Unknown to me, a young, unmarried woman who was pregnant had been invited to attend by a Christian friend. The girl was beside herself with worry and really didn't fancy sitting in a religious meeting at that point of her dilemma. Having already made up her mind to have an abortion, she was impatient to keep her doctor's appointment that very afternoon. She told me afterwards she felt out of place among all the bright-faced women who seemed to have their lives so very much together. She very definitely identified with the man sitting outside the temple gate, asking to be noticed but not really expecting anyone to give her anything that would make any practical difference to her desperate plight. She slumped miserably in her seat, wishing it was all over.

But something that was said that morning convinced this young woman she needed to become a follower of Jesus. Bowing her head quietly just where she sat, she asked the Lord to forgive her and be her Savior and Lord. At that moment she stood up spiritually on her own two feet and took one giant step forward. She decided not to keep that vital doctor's appointment. Somehow, with God helping her, she would have her baby. Somehow God and she would cope.

How do I know all of this? Because she sent me the photo of her beautiful eighteen-month-old daughter and told me the story herself!

Learning to See

Like Peter and John, we can give a helping hand to people with crippling problems like this. In His name and power we can reach out and help them onto their feet. But first we need to ask God for the ability to see the problems in the first place! For so many of us, like people coming to the temple through the Beautiful gate, walk right past the crippled beggars outside!

Why do we do this? Is it because we have to get to the church on time? Maybe the program awaits us and has become all-important—even more important than people whom God spontaneously sends our way. We so seldom even see the need right under our nose!

Once I got caught up in running a youth program. The kids, being what they were, were giving me quite enough to cope with without going out of my way to ask for *more* responsibilities. After all, I was putting in hours and hours of effort, above and beyond the call of duty. Almost every evening, as I drove the country lanes to pick up teenagers for the "youth time" at our house, I would pass a farmer's wife toiling up the hill toward her tiny home after work. She looked tired and discouraged. I felt guilty passing her by because I knew I should offer her a ride. But what if she had problems? She certainly looked unhappy. I would have to "work" at making her my friend, and quite frankly I didn't want to make the effort.

One day, however, my conscience got the better of me and I stopped. She gratefully accepted my offer of a ride, got into the van, and began to chat away about all sorts of things. I was extremely grateful that she wasn't suicidal, apparently had a good marriage, and appeared moderately happy! There was no need after all, I assured myself, for me to have worried about her.

We arrived at this woman's home and we said goodbye to each other. Everything seemed fine. But as I drove away, I had the uneasiest feeling that something was wrong. And then I realized what it was! Even though this young woman appeared perfectly whole on the outside, she had made it pretty clear in the brief time with me that she was struck with the most paralyzing spiritual disease she could possibly have—and didn't even know it! Her soul was sick because she didn't know Jesus. I knew Him and also knew the cure for her spiritual malady. I could help her.

"But, God," I remember objecting, "surely you don't expect me to attend to *every* cripple in the world!" "No," I seemed to hear Him answer, "just the ones right under your nose." How glad I was that I listened to the internal prompting of God and stopped again to help that young mother. It didn't take long to answer her questions and lead her to faith in Christ.

As you go in and out of the "gates" of your Christian responsibilities, make sure people matter first, even before programs or schedules. How many times do we ride off to church without ever inviting the "farmer's wife" across the street to come along? Why do we wait to see people in spiritual "rags" before we introduce them to Christ?

Crippled Christians

This spiritual blindness to spiritually crippled people manifests itself in all sorts of ways. Standing at the front of a church after a meeting in which I had poured out my heart concerning the need to accept Christ, I watched a shy inquirer hesitantly approaching me down the aisle, only to be almost mown down by a busy, bright believer who literally pushed the inquirer aside. The believer wanted to tell me she was going to England for a vacation and wanted to know some good churches to attend! She had, alas, little sensitivity to the "crippled" lady backing down the aisle and obviously feeling a little foolish for daring to come to the front in the first place!

You see, we not only have the problem of crippled unbelievers needing Christ; we have the problem of crippled

Christians, too! Long before he encountered the beggar at the Beautiful gate, Peter had known what it was like to be a believer crippled by the weaknesses of his own personality. After he had denied the Lord Jesus in the high priest's courtyard, he picked up crutches instead of asking God's help. He began to lean on his friends again, instead of on the Lord. He returned to the old, familiar stomping grounds of Galilee, to his fishing nets and his family. Later, Jesus lovingly and gently took those crutches away from His disciple and helped Peter walk on his own. But Peter never forgot what it was like to be crippled by failure. He knew by experience that Christ could reach out His helping hand to heal any kind of spiritual cripple—and send anyone on his way rejoicing!

What crutches do we reach for when we fall as Christians and cripple ourselves? The crutch of old friendships we left behind when we first came to faith? Do we run back to the bar or pick up the phone to the partner we used to live with? Crutches come in different shapes and sizes—they can even be "good" things such as too many Bible studies or meetings that prevent us getting involved in people's lives.

God hates to see His followers trying to keep up with Him because they are hobbling along on spiritual crutches! That brings neither honor nor glory to the One who has released us to walk free. Paul says that Jesus Christ has called us to live like kings (Rom. 5:17), not cripples!

Look at Peter—healed from his crippling fall, ready and willing to help someone else up onto his feet. Peter, filled with concern and compassion, began to minister to the poor man at the temple gate. But then, cripples have a special empathy with other cripples—and anyway, love always takes the initiative.

What I Have, I Give

It's important that we take the initiative as Peter did. Peter and John told the crippled man to "look at" them. Love stops, stoops, and says, "Jesus won't let me walk past you. I don't have the ability to give you all that you want, but I can give you some of the things you need!" "What I have I give you," said Peter. Now, all of us can say that!

But this is exactly the place that many of us have problems helping people. Because we can't do *all* the things that they need, we tend to do *none* of the things. Years ago, when I taught kindergarten in the big seaport of Liverpool, I became aware of the older brothers and sisters of the children I was teaching.

They were a needy bunch of youngsters. Some were crippled by drugs, pushing dope on anyone who would buy it from them. Young brothers and sisters and even mothers and fathers became entangled in the dangerous game. Some of the really young children went with their parents to the pub to drink all night, often cutting school and joining up with vicious gangs in the neighborhood. They needed youth clubs and counseling, reading classes, and help in finding jobs. Drug rehabilitation was a desperate need.

But I was just one young female teacher, and a novice at that. I felt absolutely helpless. What ever could I do? Because I couldn't do all that they needed, I was very tempted to do nothing at all.

But that is not the way to go. Peter gave the man what he could, not what he couldn't, and we can all start there! I decided that I would give the kids one night a week. With a few like-minded and concerned friends, I started a youth meeting, then got out on the streets and began to make friends with gang leaders. Soon we had their confidence, and they were attending the meetings.

Then another need became clear to me. These young folks were sixteen to nineteen years old, and many of them couldn't even read the most elementary words. How could they ever learn about God if they couldn't read their Bibles? Well, now, I was a teacher, so I reckoned I could at least do this much for them. And so another night was added to the schedule for teaching our new friends to read.

As the work grew and night after night was added to the agenda, I discovered one hundred and one things I could do for these kids that I had never even dreamed about—such as helping some of their families with eviction notices and collecting switchblades, razors, and others weapons of war from our new converts' pockets and collars—and even the toes of their shoes!

When we finally get around to saying, "What I have I give you," we will be absolutely amazed at what we discover we have to give, what happens to the crippled people we help, and what happens to ourselves in the process of giving it!

One night not long ago, a family in our church heard a terrible racket and went out to investigate. It turned out that a group of Laotian refugees had recently arrived in the area. It was the dead of winter. And one family of six had been given a hundred dollars and told they could spend the night in an empty house near where a family from our church lived. But the neighbors didn't like the intrusion one little bit, and the whole situation had deteriorated to a shouting match in the street.

The Christian family who were on the spot had a choice to make. They could ignore the racket and try to pretend people really weren't shouting obscenities at the frightened strangers. (Fortunately, not one of them could understand English!) Or they could go and welcome the family warmly, taking what they could to alleviate their needs.

The task looked gargantuan. How would they be received? How would they communicate? And if they started to help them today, what would they have to do tomorrow? How would they help them shop for food or find warmth before they froze to death?

But the family from our church did what they could, not what they couldn't. And through that family God began a wonderful work among the Laotian and Cambodian refugees in our area. Eventually a refugee center was formed and two churches planted among over five hundred friends and relatives of the refugees, who heard there was a church full of caring people in Milwaukee and came on in. Tomorrow usually looks after itself if we are faithful today.

Take Him to Church

Peter and John did what they could to help the crippled man at the Beautiful gate. Then they took him along with them into the temple. Well, to be truthful, we don't really know whether they took him or he took them! Anyway, in they went—the man walking and leaping and praising God (Acts 3:8)!

Now this, as you can well imagine, drew a crowd in no time flat. There was absolutely no mistaking the miracle. The man who had just been healed was forty years of age and probably was as much of a fixture as the temple gates themselves! "When all the people saw him walking and praising God, they recognized him as the same man who used to sit begging at the temple gate called Beautiful, and they were filled with wonder and amazement at what had happened to him" (vv. 9–10).

Taking his chance, Peter used the opportunity to preach a fine sermon to the impromptu audience, warning everyone not to credit John and himself for the miracle, but rather to give Jesus Christ the glory for it. For it was in Jesus' name and by His word that the man had been made whole, said Peter.

Peter's sermon was brief, but it was full of good facts and figures and not without considerable impact! Peter pointed out to the people that even though they had killed the Messiah, they had done so in ignorance. And he told them, "Repent, then, and turn to God, so that your sins may be wiped out, that times of refreshing may come from the Lord" (v. 19).

With such a dramatic visual aid standing right there in living color in front of them, what could the people do but believe? Not all of the audience, however, was so kindly disposed. The priests and leaders, though they couldn't possibly deny the miracle, were enraged about it all. They put the two disciples in jail for the night. But the "damage" had already been done, and the number of men who believed grew to about five thousand (see Acts 4:4). Now *that's* not a bad day's work!

It strikes me, however, that these men would not have been converted if Peter and John had left the healed man at the temple gate and not brought him inside. We need to take that lesson to heart, while at the same time making certain we never play the numbers game. We must realize that God works with "ones," but is perfectly able to multiply a bunch of ones into thousands if He so wishes. As far as He is concerned, a crowd is made up of thousands of ones, each especially precious in His sight!

But taking a newly healed person "into the temple" can be a risky thing to do! New converts tend to be very enthusiastic, and most churches aren't ready for too much overt joy!

I well remember being introduced by a brand-new Christian to a bunch of the lady's friends in this manner: "Here's Jill and the Holy Spirit!" Well, you can imagine I wasn't very thrilled with that introduction, and neither were her friends. But it certainly got their attention! New converts do have a happy knack of making us thoroughly ashamed of our staid faith. But then that is all the more reason we should take them along with us!

Of course, new converts don't always know quite how to behave in church. Stuart and I once took a bunch of street kids into church. They had never been to a service and had not even seen the inside of a church building, so they were extremely interested in everything. When the offering plate came down the row, they could not believe their luck! They all helped themselves as the plate passed them, remembering their manners and saying thank you very nicely!

No, new converts don't always know how to behave in church. But that bunch of wild street kids stayed around long enough to learn you put money *into* the offering plate and don't take it out, and that there are certain things that have to be learned from scratch if you've never been around Christians before! Those young people brought an awful lot of joy and wonder with them, and the adults in the congregation who were not intimidated by their rather strange dress learned to love, accept, and appreciate them. New believers bring new energy to the old believers, and old believers should be able to bring wisdom and experience to bear on the new. We need each other.

Perhaps Peter and John were a little embarrassed themselves at the sight of the newly healed man leaping and jumping and praising God. But embarrassed or not, they certainly did the right thing in bringing him to meet God's people in God's house.

The church doesn't need to be perfect. Not everyone in the congregation that day was lost in wonder, love, and praise! Some of the most prominent leaders laid hands on the apostles and put them in jail before the last hymn of the service had even been announced. But God doesn't say we must only worship if *all* the people in church are nice. He says, "Worship Me anyway, and I expect you to be in My house at the appropriate time!"

The apostles must have known they were taking a risk meeting as openly as they were doing in Solomon's Colonnade; after all, the enemies of Jesus were still very much in evidence. The courage of Peter and John has been mirrored down the centuries, as people of God in many countries where Christians are persecuted have braved the opposition and "gone to church" anyway, whatever the consequences.

Getting Inside the Gates

Another reason it's important to take new converts with us to church is to help them overcome initial obstacles—such as"getting inside the gates"! Sometimes a church service or a bunch of Christians can be extremely intimidating to someone who has lived all his or her life on the other side of the spiritual tracks!

Ben Haden, now a Presbyterian minister of some repute, was raised outside the church and not converted until he was almost thirty years of age. And he says he really had to struggle to identify with fellow believers: "Even when I went to seminary, I didn't have the slightest desire to be a pastor. I was interested in evangelism. I didn't like Christians! In fact, I think Christians are an acquired taste. You learn to like them. But for me, it didn't come naturally" (*Leadership* Magazine, Summer 1986, Vol. VII No. 3).

I was struck by Ben's statement, "I think Christians are an acquired taste!" I must confess to feeling the same way sometimes. Often people who profess nothing spiritual at all can behave in a more wholesome manner than those who seem to have known Christ forever!

Yes, it was just as well Peter and John took their new convert with them into the temple. That way they could try to explain to him the religious people they found there!

One of the most difficult things to explain to anyone is the behavior of Christian people who are not behaving! Which of us has not cringed to see the photo of some prominent preacher's wife pictured alone because her husband has run off with the woman he was counseling—or tried to explain to other basketball players the bad language exploding out of a professing Christian's mouth when he was bumped under the basket?

New believers need to grow, and they cannot do it outside the fellowship of Christians, so we must bring them to church. And we'd better keep a hand on them until they have fully understood that all sorts and conditions of men go into the temple to pray!

There does come a time, though, when we have to encourage the new converts to cope with such unpleasant discoveries for themselves. At first, they will need our explanations, and it's fine to let them hang onto us a little while until strength comes into their ankles. But the Holy Spirit has His own ways of helping new believers through their people disappointments!

I well remember hanging on with all my might to the sweet girl who led me to Jesus Christ. There came a time, however, when God took her out of my life and I was left on my own. The wisdom needed to know when to stop depending on someone or when gently to pry a loved person's fingers from your life comes from above. Only God can help us with that one.

My friend Janet had the God-given wisdom to leave me to swim on my own, once she had seen my initial capabilities as I splashed around in the shallows of my Christian faith. I know what it is to swallow water and think I'm drowning, but I'm here to tell the tale. New converts, like newborn babies, are a lot tougher than they look! And God has His own ways of taking our water wings away from us when we really don't need them anymore!

See what happened to our happy convert? One moment they were all standing together in the middle of a kind crowd who were thrilled to bits about everything that had happened to him—a crowd, moreover, who believed the apostles' message for themselves. The very next minute, the kind crowd had melted away and an extremely ugly one had replaced it. The apostles were arrested, and the healed man must have wondered if the soldiers would come back and arrest him, too! Now, I'm sure you'll admit that's quite a lot of trauma for anyone to cope with all in one day! He seems to have handled it very well, though—for the next day he was back at the temple to stand with Peter and John before the Sanhedrin.

What Happens to Former Cripples?

When I first became a Christian, I was totally surprised to find that not everyone was as happy about my conversion as I was. In fact, some of my best friends who were not believers were appalled when I told them what had happened to me. They explained to me, in effect, that cripples were cripples, and that anyone who started to leap around praising God and saying she wasn't a cripple anymore because Jesus had saved her was weird—a religious fanatic.

I guess my friends were used to my sitting happily enough outside the temple gates, and that's how they liked me! They were too embarrassed to see me "inside" Christianity, and they couldn't handle it. That was all right with me at first because God had given me new Christian friends to lean on. It wasn't until "Peter and John" were torn from my grasp when the semester ended at college that I found I couldn't draw on the strength my new Christian relationships afforded me anymore. I had been merrily hanging on to my newfound friends with all my might, listening to all they could tell me about Jesus. But then the time came to return to my hometown, where I doubted there were any disciples at all! And even if they did exist, I thought miserably, how ever would I find them?

Back home most of my fears were realized. No one was expecting a former cripple to walk back into their lives. They were not expecting one at the yacht club or the tennis courts or in the pubs! One or two of my friends were genuinely glad for me, and they were the ones I found easy to introduce to Jesus. But others near and dear to me could not for the life of them understand what had happened. Most were disappointed I had not come home from school to paint the town red as usual!

I realize now that such a radical change in someone's character can be an extremely threatening thing for others. But when the dawn has broken after a dark night in your soul, when you have been let into the secret of how it happened and, what's more, how it could happen to others, what do you do? That's right, you tell people about it, whether or not they want to hear it and whether or not anyone else helps you to do it!

The day after the crippled man was healed, Peter and John were released from jail and dragged into the middle of a most august company: "Annas the high priest was there, and so were Caiaphas, John, Alexander and the other men of the high priest's family" (Acts 4:6). Peter was fully aware that the last time he had seen Caiaphas was the night he had run away from Jesus in the garden of Gethsemane. The man whose ear he had lopped off with his sword was doubtless there as well!

This time, Peter determined to make up for his past failures. When he was asked, "By what power or what name did you do this?" (v. 7), he took off and boldly preached a short, sharp sermon ending up with the grand statement, "Salvation is found in no one else, for there is no other name (but Jesus) under heaven given to men by which we must be saved" (v. 12). Now this, you will agree, was quite a different Peter than we've known. But then he was "filled with the Holy Spirit" (v. 8)—and remember, that's what makes the difference! When we're filled with our own importance or our own strength and resolve, we'll be sure to end up denying our faith. But oh, when we're filled with the Holy Spirit, it's a whole new ball game!

The next verse is perhaps one of my favorite verses in the whole Bible: "When they saw the courage of Peter and John and realized that they were unschooled, ordinary men, they were astonished and they took note that these men had been with Jesus" (v. 13). I love it! When "unschooled ordinary men" have "been with Jesus" and are "filled with the Holy Spirit," the sky's the limit. Even a night in jail isn't going to dampen their enthusiasm. And the result will be an incredible boldness of speech and conviction of words!

But it was not only the boldness of Peter and John that stopped the religious hierarchy dead in their tracks; it was the sight of the man who had been healed. They knew as well as anyone else that this man *should* have been sitting in his usual place at the Beautiful gate, begging, yet here he was standing with Peter and John! That sort of evidence is pretty compelling! What could they say? Apparently nothing! (v. 14). So they talked agitatedly among themselves. Deciding they couldn't possibly deny the fact of the miracle and seeing that the whole of Jerusalem was buzzing about it, they decided they would threaten Peter and John and warn them to watch their step. The answer to that was predictable. Peter and John replied, "Judge for yourselves whether it is right in God's sight to obey you rather than God. For we cannot help speaking about what we have seen and heard" (vv. 19–20).

When Peter and John were released, they returned to the other disciples and told them the whole story. What joy there was among the community; they all joined together in a great paean of praise! Then they prayed for more strength and courage to witness boldly in Jerusalem, whatever the cost. When they had finished praying, "the place where they were meeting was shaken. And they were all filled with the Holy Spirit and spoke the word of God boldly" (v. 31).

On Their Own Two Feet

But what of the crippled man? Don't let us forget we left him standing with Peter and John in the middle of the high priest's entourage! He didn't need to be there. You know, the night the apostles were put in jail, he no doubt returned home to spend an incredible evening running all over town, showing off his two new legs. He was healed, he was free, and he didn't need to put himself in jeopardy by turning up at the temple again just as Peter and John were hauled out of prison!

Oh, but I believe he wanted to be there. He was probably pretty sure he couldn't say anything to help. But at least he could just stand up on his new ankles, and perhaps his mere presence would be enough in itself to lend some weight to their defense! Indeed, it was enough. What joy Peter and John must have experienced when they saw their new friend! And greater their joy when he did not rush over and cling to them again as he had done the day before. Now he was standing solidly on his own two feet!

In John's words borrowed from another occasion, the apostles could have said, "I have no greater joy than to hear that my children are walking in the truth" (3 John 4). I have known that joy, too. To pass by the bedroom door and see a child kneeling by the bed without being told to, to listen to a teenaged daughter tell me she had said no when the drugs were passed around—that's a joy that is quite unique and altogether wonderful! To see a newly converted young wife in church instead of at a "swinger's" party as had been her habit—that's all joy. Or to hear about a husband who has struggled with the bottle but who is still dry after two years—that's worth it all!

The problem arises when, to fulfill some of our own needs, we keep people clinging to us—spiritually dependent. This doesn't help us or them! Only the Holy Spirit can give us the discernment to know when to help the new believer to stand on his own two feet.

We probably should ask ourselves some hard questions about our relationship with those we have helped in the Christian life—questions such as, "Do I get a kick out of the fact that so-and-so always calls me when he's got a problem?" or "Does it massage my ego to hear her telling someone else what a blessing I've been in her life?" In truth, we should be helping others to pick up the phone to Jesus—not to us—as soon as they need an answer to a question. And we should also caution the grateful ones against giving us the credit for the things that God has wrought in their lives! The need to be needed can make us tie a person to our spiritual apron strings, creating a parent-child dependency far beyond the necessary time it takes to wean a spiritual infant. There must be caution against controlling anyone in any way for our own satisfaction.

Notice how short a time it took for the crippled man to be "off and running"! We need to be careful not to be locked in to this or that method of discipling others. As soon as the new believer has strength in his ankles, he or she should be left to stand on his own.

A girl I once led to Christ told me she was struggling to get "free" from the "hold" I had on her. This time it was not a question of her holding on to me, but rather of my holding on to her! I had thoroughly enjoyed the role I had come to play in her life—advising her about her friendships, hearing her recite her Bible verses, meeting early each morning to show her how to find her way around her Bible. But I hadn't realized I was holding her back! She had the courage to tell me she needed to cut those apron strings and make her own mistakes. "Let me stand or fall on my own, Jill," she said. As soon as we had broken the dependence, she took off like a rocket, and God began to use her in an extraordinary way.

Breaking the dependence factor doesn't mean breaking a relationship, either. This girl and I became firm friends once I'd "given her up." The situation was almost like that of a mother who gives up her own child to independence and young adulthood, thereby opening the way for friendship on an altogether different level—as equals!

Beggars and Healers

So I identify with Peter and John in their desire to do the most helpful things for the crippled man, but I also identify with the crippled man himself. When I remember the new joy of meeting Jesus—and I try to remember that regularly—I see myself as that crippled man clutching my begging bowl and trying to get people's attention. I cried out to all sorts and manner of people passing by my life just like he did, holding up my little begging bowl, hoping someone would give me something, but not really expecting anything to make a difference. One day a young girl pointed me to the only One that could do the only thing that would really count. Jesus, she told me, would not fill my bowl, but rather declare it unnecessary. He would tell me to leave my bowl outside the temple and to rise up and follow Him.

Where are you sitting as you read these pages? If you are a Christian it may be that you have some crutches you need to throw away. On the other hand, you may find yourself outside the gate of Christianity. Perhaps you are not a believer at all. Do you know people like Peter and John who regularly walk past you to church? Do you wish they would stop just once and invite you to go with them? Are your feet hobbled by the habits of years—perhaps forty years? Maybe you fear the only place you will ever be is at the gateway to this wonderful life.

Listen, Jesus is alive. He tells you He loves you. He reaches out His hand and offers it to you. Let me be a Peter today and tell you what He did for me—the chance was mine and I took it. Today, the choice is yours—why don't you take it, too!

My Begging Bowl

Help me, Jesus; see me begging here,
crooked woman that I am, hobbled by my habits,
paralyzed by thought of pain I've caused the ones I love. . . .
See me Jesus; stop and fill my begging bowl!

Help me, Jesus; see my crooked life.
Know the twisted framework of my years,
My struggle to get up and walk away from past mistakes.
Look on me in my misery—beggar that I am!
See me Jesus, stop and fill my begging bowl.

See ME, crippled woman that you are.
A crippled God hung crooked on a crooked cross—

broken, My body slumped against the wood
outside the gate called Beautiful.
There they carried Me, to hang up wet
with blood of love, to dry by midday sun
'til skin like parchment red broke free from flesh.

Well do I know the uselessness of ordering hand and feet
to help Myself and cease the agony—
only to find them hammered into place
like a bad dream, demanding to be spoiled
by dawn's sweet light.

Sweet beggar—I'll not fill your bowl
and leave you beggar still!
A greater gift I give to thee: See, take My hand;
rise up and walk with spirituality.
God did this on Easter day for Me,
Made straight My body by His resurrection power.
I left My mat in hell—and ran to meet you here.

My crippled child of love, "Be straight"—
I bid you rise and tell your world of ME!!
Go fill their begging bowls with wealth from heaven—
a hope, light, strength, and sins forgiven!
Run now, I give My gift of life to thee.
Wait not,—
My crippled world cries on!

WORKSHEET

Chapter 7

I. Read Acts 4:23–36. Then make a list of ten or more things you learn about Peter and John from the following verses that give you a clue as to their source of strength. (This can be done in groups of twos or threes and then shared.)

Verse 23
Verse 24
Verses 25–26
Verses 27–28
Verse 29
Verse 30
Verse 31
Verse 32
Verse 33
Verse 34

II. Have you ever been a crippled Christian? If so, what crutches did you use? How did God heal you—or how is He healing you now?

III. What one thing have you learned from this study or have you been reminded of that will help you to be a blessing to spiritually crippled people—both Christians and non-Christians?

IV. PRAYERTIME:

a. Praise God for helping us to straighten out our characters and for making us whole.
b. Praise God for the Peters and Johns of this world who stop and attend to the crippled world's needs.

c. Pray for people who are looking for spiritual relief in the wrong places or from the wrong people.
d. Pray for the leaders of the church.
e. Pray for believers who lean on crutches of one sort or another.
f. Pray for yourself and any "crippling" problems in your own life.

Chapter 8

PIGS

Acts 10:9–16

About noon the following day as they were approaching the city, Peter went up on the roof to pray. He became hungry and wanted something to eat, and while the meal was being prepared, he fell into a trance. He saw heaven opened and something like a large sheet being let down to earth by its four corners. It contained all kinds of four-footed animals, as well as reptiles of the earth and birds of the air. Then a voice told him, "Get up, Peter. Kill and eat." "Surely not, Lord!" Peter replied. "I have never eaten anything impure or unclean." The voice spoke to him a second time, "Do not call anything impure that God has made clean." This happened three times, and immediately the sheet was taken back to heaven.

Acts 10:9–16

The Pigs of Prejudice

God uses people we know and love and people we hardly know at all to teach us "people" lessons. He also uses people we like and people we dislike—and occasionally even folks we despise—to turn us around in a whole new direction.

Someone has said, you can choose your friends, but you can't choose your relatives! That I suppose is true. But I have found out you can't choose your friends, your relatives, or even your enemies if you follow Jesus. That's because He chooses them for you! And when that happens, as Peter discovered, there can be no room in your life for the pigs of prejudice!

Those of us who take pride in the fact that we are not prejudiced usually find out that we are! I used to think I was only prejudiced against people who were prejudiced. At the same time, true to my upbringing, I believed that middle-class English people just didn't mix with "lower-class" English people; "It just isn't done," as we British folk say. I would never have voiced the words *common* or *unclean* out loud, but then I didn't have to do anything about my prejudices in those days. I could live in my big house, play tennis at the most prestigious club, and choose like-minded (and prejudiced) friends!

Then I found the Lord—and discovered He kept strange company. Soon I was seeing my prejudices in a whole new light. Call it vision if you will—a vision of Him that gave me a vision of them and a vision of me! This all drew attention to the fact that I needed to deal with my judgmental attitudes.

This was the same lesson Peter learned while he was visiting some Christian brothers at Joppa and staying with Simon the tanner. He went up to the top of the house while the meal was being prepared. And even though he was hungry, he still managed to fall asleep! The Lord, never fazed by the way we fall asleep on Him, walked into Peter's dreams and met him there. He showed him some "pigs in a blanket." (Talk about the way to a man's heart being through his stomach!)

In this dream, Peter saw a sheet coming down from heaven

containing a variety of animals. Some were "clean" animals—meaning quadrupeds that had cloven hooves and chewed the cud and were therefore permitted to be eaten by the Israelites. The others, however, were "unclean" animals forbidden to the Jews by their law—including pigs.

"Get up, Peter. Kill and eat," the Lord said to him.

"Surely not, Lord!" Peter protested. "I have never eaten anything impure or unclean."

"Do not call anything impure that God has made clean," replied Jesus (Acts 10:13–15).

Now, it's important to realize that the people of Israel were extremely careful about their eating habits. They were not supposed to buy any bread or milk from the Gentiles or even to sit at table with them, for fear case they might eat "unclean" meat and defile themselves. To a good Jew like Peter, the idea of eating an "unclean" animal—especially at the Lord's bidding—was shocking!

But the application of Peter's vision was abundantly clear. God made no distinction between people, even between Jews and non-Jews. The gospel was to be given to the Gentiles. The Lord knew that if they were given the chance, they would receive the Good News and respond. God would cleanse and accept them just as He had the Jews, and He expected His followers to accept them, too. As Paul would write later, in Christ there was to be neither Jew nor Greek, slave nor free, male nor female. All were to be one in Christ Jesus (see Gal. 3:28).

The Lord went on to tell Peter that some Gentile men were actually on their way to escort him to a Gentile home. He was to go with them, eat Gentile food, and sleep on a Gentile bed. Even as the Lord spoke to Peter, the men He was speaking about arrived at his house, and suddenly Peter was wide awake! Inviting them to stay for the night, he told them he would go to their master's house the next day. I'm sure the Gentile messengers had their own prejudice to overcome, but they accepted the kind offer of hospitality and the following day escorted Peter and some Christian brothers to the house of Cornelius.

Cornelius was waiting for them anxiously. We are told that he was a centurion of high rank in what was known as the Italian Regiment, and that he was a good man. The good things Cornelius had done, such as giving generously to those in need, sprang from his naturally noble character. Cornelius was also a religious man—or at least a sincere seeker. He obviously had no sympathy with the religious fables and sensual indulgences of his time. And he seemed to attribute to the Jewish faith a pure and undefiled concept of God; at least he had apparently adopted some of the features of the Jewish faith such as prayer, fasting, and alms giving.

One very memorable day—the day before Peter had his vision on the rooftop—good Cornelius had set apart a period for earnest inquiry about the way of salvation. He had received a very dramatic answer from heaven. And that is when he had sent for Peter.

A man or woman sincerely responding to the light he or she has received is bound to receive more light until he or she "sees" the truth as it is in Jesus. However, that person needs a light bearer, as Peter was to Cornelius. I once asked a self-professed atheist if she would pray this prayer with me, "Lord, if You exist, show Yourself to me." She agreed to try it, even though she confessed to feeling foolish doing so. Several months later, she cautiously began to read the Gospel of Mark, and eventually she found the Lord. This young girl reminded me very much of Cornelius. She was a delightful person with everything going for her. Seeing her integrity, God sent her a light bearer—me, in this instance—to explain the gospel more fully.

Peter finally arrived at Cornelius' home to discover a houseful of relatives and friends waiting eagerly for him. Now, this was not surprising. When a man you love and admire has been visited by an angel who tells him to send for a man who has a message from God, you'd want to be there, too! As Peter came into the house, Cornelius fell down at his feet to worship him. But Peter picked the Roman back up, saying "Stand up . . . I am only a man myself" (v. 26). Then he went inside the house with Cornelius.

What a moment for the world. It was by far the greatest "giant step" ever taken for mankind—even greater than the first step on the moon! If Peter had not overcome his prejudice and stepped inside that house, Gentiles like you and me might never be Christians today. I am so glad he did!

Having introduced himself to the assembled crowd, Peter went on to explain his ambivalence honestly. "You are well aware that it is against our law for a Jew to associate with a Gentile or to visit him. But God has shown me that I should not call any man impure or unclean. So when I was sent for, I came without raising any objection. May I ask why you sent for me?" (vv. 28–29).

Then Cornelius encouraged Peter to deliver his message. "Now we are all here in the presence of God to listen to everything the Lord has commanded you to tell us," he said (v. 33).

And Peter, full of wonder, exclaimed, "I now realize how true it is that God does not show favoritism but accepts men from every nation who fear him and do what is right" (vv. 34–35).

Peter had discovered the stupendous fact that God isn't prejudiced. If we are to be like God, then, we must not be a respecter of persons, either. But that is definitely easier said than done!

Peter went on to preach up a storm about Jesus of Nazareth. He explained that he and the other apostles were eyewitnesses of Jesus' works and miracles. He told his little congregation that unfortunately his own people had slaughtered Jesus and hung Him on a cross, but that on the third day God had raised Him from the dead. The apostles had seen the Lord and talked with Him, and now they had been commissioned to tell His story.

"All the prophets testify about him that everyone who believes in him receives forgiveness of sins through his name," Peter finished quietly (v. 43), assuring them that whoever believed in Him—whatever creed, color, culture, or clime—would be saved.

Peter didn't have time to finish his sermon before the Holy Spirit fell on them all and the new converts, filled with the Holy Ghost, began to praise and magnify the Lord. There was nothing to stop the new Gentile believers from being baptized. And after that, Peter and his friends stayed around for a few days, confirming the new Christians in their faith.

Defining Prejudice

I wonder just how many Corneliuses are waiting for us to knock upon their doors? How many lovely, noble unbelievers worry and wonder all alone in their quiet places, hoping somehow God will give them answers to their many questions? And how many of us are sleeping our way through the day of salvation to suppertime—hungry not for souls, but merely for some temporal satisfaction?

Our lethargy is caused by prejudice! Let's define the pig so we will recognize it when we hear it grunt, lay it on the dinner table of truth, and be done with it!

The dictionary defines prejudice as "a judgment or opinion held in disregard of the facts that contradict it" or "a preconceived idea, usually unfavorable." It's a judgment or opinion formed before the case is heard! To judge a person without a fair hearing, with partiality, breeds suspicion, intolerance, and the hatred of those who are different.

Prejudice manifests itself in a variety of ways. Let me give you some examples.

When we were planning to immigrate to the United States, I tried to prepare our three grade-schoolers for the transition. I wanted to make them aware that differences sometimes breed prejudice. "The other boys and girls may laugh at your British accent," I warned them. "Just remember though," Stuart chipped in, grinning, "*they* have the accent; you don't!"

We laughed then, although I still wondered how our children would cope. But when the time came, to my amazement and pleasure, the prejudice I had warned our children about never materialized. Everyone was delighted with them and with their English accents—which, incidentally, lasted all of four weeks! The Briscoe children were the wonder of the community! People would hide behind pillars at the church just to hear them talk!

It was for this reason that I felt I could assure the wife of a new pastor from the deep South not to worry about the adjustment her four lively boys would have to make. "People were wonderful to our kids," I assured her. "You'll see, they will be wonderful to yours, too." Alas, I couldn't have been more wrong. I could hardly believe the abuse those boys had to bear. They were laughed at and ridiculed because of their southern accents, and they were left out of lots of activities. I could not for the life of me understand this prejudice, but then I was from England, not Mississippi or South Carolina!

Having traveled the world, I don't have much trouble coming up with plenty of examples of prejudice outside this country. Five weeks in South Africa graphically highlighted the black-white problem, while a spell in my own home capital of London shocked me as I witnessed racial violence brought about by the unrestricted immigration policies at the time.

Such prejudices are totally condemned by the Lord, and partiality is in fact forbidden. Leviticus 19:15 gives us a crystal-clear directive: "Do not pervert justice; do not show partiality to the poor or favoritism to the great, but judge your neighbor fairly." In other words, we are not to judge others at all! As Peter reminded his hearers (and, no doubt, himself), "[Jesus] commanded us to preach to the people and to testify that he is the one whom God appointed as judge of the living and the dead" (Acts 10–42). But so often we are far too happy to let Him judge the dead while we take it upon ourselves to judge the living for Him!

James, the brother of our Lord, echoed Leviticus when he talked about a kind of prejudice we can all relate to. He warned us not to show partiality to the rich man and ignore the poor man (James 2:1–4). In our churches there is often another twist to that—we show partiality to those we consider spiritually rich, while ignoring the spiritually poor.

When I arrive somewhere to speak at a convention, I make

my way to the registration table like everyone else. All too often, I find myself being pushed and pulled about by all the other ladies in line who, like me, want to get registered and settled into their rooms before the meeting begins. It's every woman for herself.

But then, suddenly, someone recognizes me as the speaker, and an immediate transformation takes place. People begin to back away respectfully, giving me room to breathe. The rather rude lady in front or behind, who has been shouldering me roughly out of the way a moment before, smiles sweetly and whips out one of my books for me to autograph! Partiality wins the day! But this ought not to be.

Now, I am obviously not suggesting that we should treat speakers as rudely as we treat ordinary conference attenders! Rather, we should treat everyone—speakers and listeners alike—with the same, unprejudiced respect. For that, I believe, is what the Lord commands.

The Problem of Principle

But why do we have so much trouble avoiding prejudice in ourselves and others? One reason is that we can be so conditioned by our cultural traditions and even our strong religious principles that we cannot see beyond them.

One reason it was hard for Peter to treat all men as equals was that he was a good Jew. Peter was a man of principle, and men of principle can oftentimes be men of rigidity. Our principles and traditions can make us unable to cope with changes because we don't want to compromise. We may come to view change as a threat to our very belief system.

Peter had to learn that his religious tradition—in this case, the keeping of the oral law and the interpretation of it concerning his eating habits—could well conflict with the spirit of the law as Jesus had given it to them. The important thing at this moment of time was that the Gentiles might have the chance to hear the gospel, not that Peter might watch his diet! Truth needed to take precedent over the tradition of the elders and Peter's own religious heritage.

The very same issue came up at a much later date, when Paul and Barnabas traveled up to Jerusalem to report the conversion of the Gentiles. In Jerusalem there were certain believers from the sect of the Pharisees who challenged Paul and Barnabas about the behavior of the new converts, insisting that they be made to keep the Mosaic law. After a lot of debate and argument, it was Peter who stood up to the dissenting party and defended the new converts by saying, "God, who knows the heart, showed that he accepted them by giving the Holy Spirit to them, just as he did to us. He made no distinction between us and them, for he purified their hearts by faith. Now then, why do you try to test God by putting on the necks of the disciples a yoke that neither we nor our fathers have been able to bear?" (Acts 15:8–10).

In other words, Peter was arguing, God knows the hearts of all people—people such as Peter, Cornelius, and even the prejudiced Pharisees. Whoever seek Him with all of their hearts shall surely find Him and will be given the Holy Spirit—regardless of the restrictions of tradition.

How can we relate such a Jewish dilemma to our own culture and time? Think of the churches where the Christian gospel is faithfully preached, Lord's day after Lord's day without any real thought as to who is there to hear it.

I once belonged to such a fellowship. For many years it had been their standard practice to "feed the saints" on Sunday mornings and "preach to the sinners" on Sunday night, when their traditional "gospel" meeting was held. The problem was that the "sinners" for whom this service was provided were seldom if ever there to hear and respond to the message! Things had changed, and now in our particular location the unconverted went to church in the mornings—if they went at all!

"Why convince the convinced?" I innocently asked an elder one Sunday night after observing the small group of faithful believers who listened attentively week after week to the gospel service. (I was a pretty new Christian at the time and had lots of friends who needed Christ, few of whom I could persuade to come near the door of a church—much less a

Sunday evening gospel meeting!) The elder, somewhat piqued, replied that it was a church tradition to preach the gospel in the evening—and anyway, it had been very effective in the past.

To the elder, changing gears seemed like compromising the "truth." After all, as he said, "What happens if a stranger comes in one night? What would we say to the Lord if we hadn't prepared a message appropriate to his needs?" But the same elder seemed oblivious to the fact that strangers *were* coming in on Sunday mornings—not to mention gathering in plenty of places besides church—and they were not hearing the gospel.

It is easy to get so bogged down in external religious tradition that we lose touch with the reality behind the traditions! That is what had happened to the Jewish people in Peter's day. The Pharisees put great stress on the traditional rituals of their religion. They had so many endless rules that the people were glad to reduce their religious life to outward and literal obediences—just so they could cope with all the demands. Their thoughts could behave or misbehave at will, as long as they kept to the letter of the law.

The idea of true holiness, where so much depends on the control of the thought life, cut right across the Pharisees' religious observances. But that is exactly what Jesus had taught. Jesus had broken some of the bonds of tradition and demonstrated a life lived out of truth and based on the essence and spirit of the law.

Dead religious tradition says, "Don't think; just do the things I tell you to do. Work at looking right on the outside, and you can have a heyday on the inside!" Jesus, on the other hand, brought great attention to bear on our thought life and demanded we deal with it. In fact, He chastised the Pharisees because in their overconcern for externals they had neglected the internals: "You hypocrites! You clean the outside of the cup and dish, but inside they are full of greed and self-indulgence. . . . You are like whitewashed tombs, which look beautiful on the outside but on the inside are full of dead men's bones and everything unclean" (Matt. 23:25–26).

Peter found that his faith in Jesus demanded that he think about his traditions, not just accept them blindly! There had to be an ongoing process of sorting out what was "right" from what was "ritual." And Peter's obedience in visiting Cornelius showed he had finally grasped what his Master had been saying about true righteousness. In other words, Peter realized that to eat food prepared by his Gentile hosts would not defile him nearly so much as to allow prejudiced thoughts to keep him from doing what the Lord wanted! Prejudging another would more truly defile his spirit than would a banquet of pig meat!

One of the first things we must do to rid our lives of prejudice, then, is to learn how to think—to differentiate between tradition and truth. For tradition itself isn't bad, because tradition tries to preserve the truth. Tradition only becomes problematical when it obscures the truth it is trying to preserve or becomes a substitute for the reality it intends to convey!

When I became a believer, I wanted to join a church, so I eventually discovered a good one and became a member. It happened to be a Baptist church. It was lively and full of bright, young people. Soon I was made the local representative for the Baptist convention and threw myself into the work it involved.

Two years later, however, I was more Baptist than Christian. And I'm afraid I had become thoroughly prejudiced against all other denominations, who I felt really didn't have the "pure truth" as I believed "we" did. It was only as I got involved in nondenominational work that I realized I had allowed myself to be thoroughly sidetracked. I had learned to judge others quicker than a blink and ended up playing party politics instead of bringing in the kingdom!

Prejudice and Prayer

So how do we overcome prejudice? We need to be alert for it in our lives. And we need to learn to think—to sort out unchanging truth from dead tradition. But in order to do this, we must pray about it and ask God to help us sort out truth from His point of view.

Remember, God is never prejudiced. So it follows that the more time we spend alone with Him, the more His attitude will rub off on us!

Peter believed in prayer. But Peter also had a problem with prayer—one many of us can identify with. He just couldn't keep awake! Jesus frequently prayed all night and taught His disciples to pray, too, but Peter often found himself nodding off at the critical moment. The spirit was willing, but the flesh was weak!

But Peter didn't give up. In fact, if he had not been convinced that prayer was vital, I doubt he could ever have overcome his prejudice. We know that he regularly practiced prayer (see Acts 3:1), although when he got hungry or tired the same old struggle would begin all over again. By the time the Lord caught Peter sleeping on the job on Simon's rooftop, the habit of prayer had become so ingrained that he was able to "talk" through the whole area of prejudice with the Lord even while he was asleep!

We must practice vital prayer all the time so that it becomes an unconscious habit—just as it did with Peter. For it will be in prayer that the Lord will face us with our prejudices and show us how we can overcome them.

Most of us, like Peter, tend to sleep our way through the issues of life. Jesus may even be transfigured before us, as He was before Peter, and we can slumber the opportunity away (Luke 9:32). Or the cross may be just around the corner of tomorrow, and we may be deliberately forgetful of our spiritual disciplines (Matt. 26:40). It may be we are more concerned with our physical well-being or our emotional health or even our spiritual temperature to take any notice of the people outside our safe circle of Christian friends—even the Corneliuses who are searching for the truth we could share with them. Some of us could even be in "prison" and have to have an angel of God poke us in the ribs to wake us up to an opportunity to escape (Acts 12:6–8)!

I must say I am encouraged to know that Peter slept through

all of the above—because I, too, struggle with the same problem. It is so much easier to sleep than to struggle! It's also good to know, however, that God woke Peter up every time! Real prayer to a real God wakes us up to the real issues that must be dealt with in a real way, and it's through our obedience to His commands that real results are achieved.

So it eventually all comes back to that old issue of obedience. Peter had a choice—a choice to battle his problem of prejudice out in prayer. He could listen to the Lord and welcome Gentiles into his house or he could tell them to go and find a motel down the road! Having wrestled through the problem in prayer, Peter began to overcome a very real prejudice. He demonstrated the Spirit of his Lord and reached out to those who did not know Christ.

Making Contact

In Peter's case, it was contact with the very people he was prejudiced against that helped him overcome his prejudice! And that is true in many situations.

Who are you prejudiced against? What are you prejudiced about? Do you judge some people "common" and "unclean"? Have you prejudged situations or individuals to such a degree that you have isolated and insulated yourselves from all contact with them?

If so, contact must be made in order for prejudice to be eliminated. And this means plans have to be put into effect to make that contact happen.

A couple of decades ago, the phrase "generation gap" was very familiar to all of us. The young people of the 1960s felt older people didn't understand them. And the older people freely admitted that the young people of the day were a total mystery to them—almost like creatures from another planet! A huge communication gap yawned between the generations. And this was true within the church as well as outside it; the generation gap permeated fellowships of believers all over the land.

It was during this turbulent time that our family came to America to pastor our church in Milwaukee. The "Jesus Movement," in which enterprising Christians won many so-called "hippies" and "flower children" to Christ, had run its course, and now these new converts from the "counterculture" were beginning to think about coming to church. But the church by and large was not very happy to have them come, for they still dressed and acted differently from the average churchgoer.

The weeds of prejudice spread prolifically in such a no man's land. Watered by mistrust and misinformation, they grew so tall that they made it very difficult for anyone to see across that jungle tract.

In our church, through the work of a very dedicated couple, we had an influx of these so-called "Jesus people," and a thoroughly conservative member of our fellowship came to talk to my husband about the situation. "You must keep these hippies separate from our kids," he said firmly. He could well have added, "especially mine!" This man's fear was understandable, but we believed it was unfounded. We had come to know the converted "flower people," and we believed they would do the church kids nothing but good once they got to know each other.

My husband explained this to the concerned church member. He looked a little disappointed that we were not willing to isolate the new people, but at the same time he was willing to admit that the problem lay not so much in the kids' relationships with each other but rather in the huge generation gap between parents and children.

Out of this exchange, my husband and this man crafted a special class entitled "Generation Bridge." It was designed to bring old and young together. We decided that the "way out" and the "way in," the liberal and the conservative, and especially the young and the old would take part together.

We shared the idea with the congregation and said that participation in the class would be by invitation only. This of course ensured that a good number immediately wanted to participate! We then divided the class into pairs, taking care to match up opposites. We gave them the Book of James to study and left them to lead it themselves, pair by pair.

At the end of three months, the participants didn't want to stop, but there was already a long waiting list for the next class! It was a full year before we disbanded the class; by then, the need had been met. An opportunity for dialogue had been provided—a place to talk together, not sharing ignorance or preconceived ideas, but studying Scripture. The Word of God does its own wonderful work where prejudice is concerned. As we try to listen to the Word of God and to each other, the Spirit will lend us His help to be "doers of the Word, and not hearers only" (James 1:22, KJV)!

Bridges over Barriers

There are as many different ways of building bridges over gaps as there are people in the world. We can create a bridge by getting to know someone whose political views conflict with ours and then trying to understand why this person feels as he or she does. Or we can join an organization knowing there are groups within it from different socioeconomic backgrounds, thus forcing ourselves to spend time with people we'd never meet in our ordinary round of life. We can always invite people home for a meal; there is no better place for meaningful, constructive dialogue than at our own firesides. Even having a free and frank exchange over lunch with an adversary on a hot issue can be an occasion for bridge building.

We can break down prejudice by initiating opportunities like these. If in fact we don't, it is very doubtful the other party will! Love always takes the initiative. And building bridges offers us a chance to really understand each other.

Take, for example, the issue of women's role in the church. I myself am still wrestling with the intricate problems surrounding this issue. There are so many thoroughly sound evangelicals on both sides of the controversy, and the biblical answers are not nearly as clear-cut as most people would like to think. Men and women I respect greatly take opposite positions about what women may or may not do in the church. We need to talk the question out. And then it may be necessary to agree to disagree, with respect for each other's honest integrity.

There are some people on both sides of the issue, however, who haven't paid much attention to the theological problems involved with the issue. These people's minds are made up, and they don't want to be confused with facts. I have found some to be rude; others are hostile, and on occasion, even verbally abusive. They are thoroughly prejudiced. They have formed their opinions before the facts are known or the case is heard, and they manifest suspicion, intolerance, and even hatred toward those whose opinions are different.

On one occasion, I was speaking to a group of both men and women. I had been invited by a particular organization to do so and had gladly accepted the challenge. A young man near the front of the auditorium waited until I was about ten minutes into my talk. Then, slowly and deliberately, he got up and walked out.

After the meeting, I happened to bump into the young man in the lobby. And although I am not a confrontational person at all, I plucked up courage to ask him why he had left the room. Something about his demeanor had told me that he was not ill or in the wrong meeting, but had been trying to make a point.

My instincts proved right. The young man was completely taken aback when I questioned him, but he admitted he had wanted to express his strong beliefs that women should not address mixed gatherings. He felt that according to Scripture I should not be doing the teaching in that seminar. As we talked, however, I discovered his feelings stemmed from a cultural experience and were subjective and biased. He had never even examined the relevant Scriptures or read the work of any of the experts who had written on either side of the issue.

I was able to stimulate and challenge him to consider studying the subject, and I assured him he would find out it was certainly not as clear-cut as he imagined. But through this experience I also learned how deeply some people feel about the issue. So my talk with the young man was an important bridge toward understanding for both of us.

Our willingness to make contact is crucial to our being able to build bridges! For when we do this in obedience to the Lord, we often find our prejudices dissolve.

For example, Peter was definitely prejudiced against Roman centurions before he received his orders to visit Cornelius. But he was "for God" and His plan and so was willing to obey. And that was a starting point!

After all, what did Peter really know about Roman centurions? How many Romans had ever been invited to dinner at Peter's house? How much meaningful dialogue had taken place? When Peter actually accepted the invitation to the Roman's house, what a blessing the whole experience turned out to be! It was Cornelius himself who helped Peter overcome his prejudice against Romans!

So often this is the case. Peter discovered that Gentiles could be courteous, hospitable, ready to listen, and eager to be taught. They could be willing to obey God—to pray and fast and give alms. Peter found to his great surprise that Gentiles could be all-right people. I'm sure the more time he spent with those folks, the more of his prejudices were laid to rest.

The Deep Roots of Prejudice

Building bridges is absolutely crucial for breaking down prejudice. But building bridges can be very hard work, for our prejudices often have very deep roots.

Not long ago, Joni Earickson Tada was slated to speak in our city. Our women's ministry board had sponsored the visit of this remarkable young woman, who is a paraplegic. Everyone worked terribly hard for a full year in preparation for the event.

As the time for Joni's visit drew near, however, one of our most capable women began to give me signals that she would not be available once the meetings began. I sensed a real disturbance in her spirit and took her out for lunch to see if she wanted to talk about it. She ended up telling me a story about her childhood.

As a little girl, my friend had ridden a school bus everyday with a severely handicapped child. He was not a pretty sight and drooled continually. She had found herself sitting next to him all the time—not because she wanted to, but because no one else wanted to, either, and being the youngest and smallest she had no option.

The handicapped boy had not been very nice to her, and ever since then she had struggled with a huge prejudice against handicapped people. She confessed she just could not bring herself to meet or interact with the hundreds of disabled people who would be around at our special event.

I encouraged this woman to use the opportunity to face her particular pig of prejudice and "eat it." And she agreed to wrestle with the problem in prayer. Later, I was not surprised to find out she had signed up for the transportation committee—a job that would involve a lot of physical contact with the very people she had prejudged all these years! Inwardly I applauded this woman's courage and obedience in facing her deep-rooted prejudice and asking God's help in overcoming her fear.

For after all, fear plays an important role in prejudice. It was fear of "contamination" that worried the strict Christian parent in our church who didn't want his children mixing with "hippies." A fear of a "takeover" by women can get to some men who are a little insecure, especially when they meet a woman with equal gifts. And the fear born from an unfortunate childhood incident can effectively build into our lives barriers of prejudice that are extremely difficult to surmount!

But then, fear is often the child of ignorance. When the barriers go up between people or communities, then the resulting isolation breeds fear. The physical barrier of the Berlin Wall that separates the East from the West is an extreme example—or the barricades across the roads in areas of Northern Ireland that effectively seal the Catholic children off from the little Protestants across the street. And there are unseen barriers like this in many communities. Wherever people grow in total ignorance of each other, a fear and prejudice can flourish that may well end in bloodshed and tears!

Christ Crosses Boundaries

It is Christ, of course, who can make the difference! Referring to the literal barrier that the Jews erected in the temple courtyard to separate Jew from Gentile, Paul remarks, "For he himself is our peace, who has made the two one and has destroyed the barrier, the dividing wall of hostility" (Eph. 2:14). It is only by understanding the universal plan of God and by asking humbly to be a part of bringing that plan into effect that the Christian can begin to understand his prejudices and work to overcome them.

If we are really to look around for an example of someone who could have had reason to be prejudiced but wasn't, we would have to look at Jesus Himself. Just think of the Incarnation. Jesus ate the food, wore the clothes, drank the water, and played the games of the people among whom He lived. He learned their culture and language and busied Himself learning their trades.

He did not prejudge the woman at the well, as His disciples most certainly did (John 4:1–30). Neither did He prejudge the woman who washed His feet with her tears and wiped them with her hair, as His host certainly did (Luke 7:36–50). He talked with the Syrophoenician woman—even healing her daughter (Mark 7:24–30)—and He ate with publicans and sinners such as Matthew (Matt. 9:9–13) and Zacchaeus (Luke 19:1–9), capturing their hearts and changing their behavior forever.

Jesus' example was radical. He allowed His disciples pick corn on the Sabbath day, a practice forbidden by the Pharisees. And He ate with ceremonially unwashed hands on another occasion. Over and over He tried to tell people to differentiate between tradition and truth—and called them to follow the truth, which abolishes prejudice.

Let God Be the Judge

Peter and you and I have a divine model, divine imperatives, and divine power to do something about our judgmental attitudes—whether they come from our backgrounds and traditions, from traumatic past experiences, or from fear of the unknown. If we are going to beat prejudice, we must know ourselves, watch ourselves, and help ourselves. But once again, we must seek the Lord's help, for prejudice is a deep-rooted thing. If Peter teaches us anything, he teaches us that one victory does not necessarily guarantee us automatic victory for the rest of our lives.

After much meaningful ministry to both Jew and Gentile, Peter found himself in a bind. Some very conservative brothers came to visit, and Peter didn't want to face their criticism. He became concerned about just what the "big shots" would say about his eating with Gentiles, and so he withdrew and ate separately with the visiting brethren. But Paul caught him compromising in the situation and wasn't a bit backward in facing him with it. Paul confronted Peter because he allowed prejudice—other people's prejudice, in this instance—to override the new principles he had learned and even taught (Gal. 2:11–14)!

It's hard to believe Peter would do this, but then the cock crows many times in a person's life, and we must remember never to say never! If we are honest, all of us care far too much what others think or say about us. Peter could have helped himself by listening to the right people, but he didn't. He should have listened to Paul, not to the group of biased visitors. We can really help ourselves by deciding to listen to people we really respect instead of to the loudest voice.

Yes, prejudice runs deep, and we may beat it at one place only to find it beating us at the next. God helped me to overcome my prejudice of kids on drugs when I worked with them. But ten years later, when my daughter wanted to date a young man who had taken drugs before he became a Christian, I balked! I can relate to you how my friend overcame her prejudice about handicapped people—thinking even as I write, "That's never been a problem for me." And yet I resist the idea of one of our children adopting a disabled child!

But what about the situation that arises when we don't struggle with our own prejudices but are the object of someone else's? How do we react when someone pre-judges us or just outright criticizes us? I've touched on my own experience over the women's issue, and there have been plenty of other situations that I could recount. After all, I'm a pastor's wife, and many people have preconceived ideas about what pastor's wives are (or should be) like!

I believe the key to both situations—our own lingering prejudices and the prejudice of others against us—can be found in 1 Corinthians 4. In this passage, the apostle Paul says,

> I care very little if I am judged by you or by any human court; indeed, I do not even judge myself. My conscience is clear, but that does not make me innocent. It is the Lord who judges me. Therefore judge nothing before the appointed time; wait till the Lord comes. He will bring to light what is hidden in darkness and will expose the motives of men's hearts (vv. 3–5).

Now, Paul did not say he cared *nothing* about what others think—that would not be right. We *should* care enough when we are criticized to examine ourselves to see if there is any truth in the accusations. But Paul has a caution even about such self-examination. He says he doesn't take too seriously other's words and doesn't even take himself too seriously. He refuses to indulge in a soul-dredging operation, but instead commits himself to the One who judges righteously and is content to rest his case until another day and time in another dimension.

In this passage, Paul effectively points out the reason that prejudice is so unfair. Only God has all the facts and knows the motives of people's hearts, which will surely be revealed one day in order for Judge Jesus to reach a just conclusion on the matter. Meanwhile, if other people suspect our motives—let them. They cannot possibly have all the relevant information necessary to judge us and therefore cannot possibly understand all the reasons we behave as we do. And so, Paul says to his readers, "judge *nothing* before the appointed time" (v. 5).

Our job is, as best as we know how, to keep our own hearts

free from prejudice. And when we find ourselves under attack from people who are prejudging us, we must be careful not to return the accusations. We are, after all, only responsible for our own reactions and responses.

The thing I love about being a Christian is that the ground is level at the foot of the cross. God is no respecter of persons, so who do we think we are showing partiality? God gifts all of us for service, and we need to realize there are no medals for gifts—only for faithfulness! We are called to be faithful stewards, not supreme court judges, and we'd better remember it!

One day Paul was hauled before the judgment seat—the *bēma*—to answer to a Roman official for his ministry. He acquitted himself well, and his case was dismissed. He was no doubt referring to that incident when he later wrote to them, "We must all appear before the judgment seat of Christ, that each one may receive what is due him for the things done while in the body, whether good or bad" (2 Cor. 5:10).

In the end, that is where it will all end and justice will be done! Wrongs will be righted and right will be rewarded. Peter and Paul will be given the martyr's crown, and you and I will have a fair trial as to how we have followed Jesus.

Years ago, I came across a poem scribbled on a piece of paper. I took it with me one year on a tour to the Holy Land, and there in Corinth I read it to the group of fellow travelers as we stood in front of the *bēma* that has been excavated there. Somehow, I believe Peter and Paul would have echoed these sentiments had they been around, but they were not. They, after all, had beaten the cock's crow for the last time and were "home." Until that time comes for us as well, we need to keep the *bēma* of Christ in mind.

When I stand at the judgment seat of Christ
   and He shows me His plan for me,
the plan of my life as it might have been,
   had He had His way, and I see
how I blocked Him here, and checked Him there
   and would not yield my will,
shall I see grief in my Savior's eyes—

grief though He loves me still?
He would have me rich, but I stand here poor,
stripped of all but His grace,
while my memory runs like a hunted thing
down the paths I can't retrace.
Then my desolate heart will well-nigh break
with tears that I cannot shed,
and I'll cover my face with my empty hands
and bow my uncrowned head.
No, Lord of the life that's left to me,
I yield it to Thy hand.
Take me, make me, mold me
to the pattern Thou hast planned.

One day I'll stand before the judgment seat of my Jesus. I don't want to have empty hands, and I don't want to have an uncrowned head. Do you?

It is fitting however, to let Peter have the last word with us.

But the day of the Lord will come like a thief.
The heavens will disappear with a roar;
the elements will be destroyed by fire,
and the earth and everything in it will be laid bare.
Since everything will be destroyed in this way,
what kind of people ought you to be?
You ought to live holy and godly lives
as you look forward to the day of God
and speed its coming.
2 Peter 3:10–12

Even so, come Lord Jesus!

AMEN.

WORKSHEET

Chapter 8

I. RECOGNIZING PREJUDICE:
   a. Review the definition of prejudice in this chapter.
   b. What are some of your prejudices?
   c. Which of Peter's problems did you relate to and why?
      Discipline in prayer
      Rigidity about religious tradition
      Aversion to certain kinds of people

II. OVERCOMING PREJUDICE: Read Luke 7:36–51.
   a. How much prejudice does Simon show and to whom?
   b. What does Jesus do about it? Say about it?
   c. What can I learn from this?

III. BEATING PREJUDICE: Read 1 Corinthians 4:1–5. Which part of this passage will help you to beat prejudice on a regular basis?

IV. PRAYERTIME:
   a. Pray about your prejudice and ask the Lord for help in overcoming it.
   b. Pray for your church that critical spirits will not cause division and hurt.
   c. Pray for world missions that wisdom will be given to bridge cross-cultural barriers.

CHRISTIAN HERALD ASSOCIATION AND ITS MINISTRIES

CHRISTIAN HERALD ASSOCIATION, founded in 1878, publishes The Christian Herald Magazine, one of the leading interdenominational religious monthlies in America. Through its wide circulation, it brings inspiring articles and the latest news of religious developments to many families. From the magazine's pages came the initiative for CHRISTIAN HERALD CHILDREN and THE BOWERY MISSION, two individually supported not-for-profit corporations.

CHRISTIAN HERALD CHILDREN, established in 1894, is the name for a unique and dynamic ministry to disadvantaged children, offering hope and opportunities which would not otherwise be available for reasons of poverty and neglect. The goal is to develop each child's potential and to demonstrate Christian compassion and understanding to children in need.

Mont Lawn is a permanent camp located in Bushkill, Pennsylvania. It is the focal point of a ministry which provides a healthful "vacation with a purpose" to children who without it would be confined to the streets of the city. Up to 1000 children between the age of 7 and 11 come to Mont Lawn each year.

Christian Herald Children maintains year-round contact with children by means of a *City Youth Ministry.* Central to its philosophy is the belief that only through sustained relationships and demonstrated concern can individual lives be truly enriched. Special emphasis is on individual guidance, spiritual and family counseling and tutoring. This follow-up ministry to inner-city children culminates for many in financial assistance toward higher education and career counseling.

THE BOWERY MISSION, located at 227 Bowery, New York City, has since 1879 been reaching out to the lost men on the Bowery, offering them what could be their last chance to rebuild their lives. Every man is fed, clothed and ministered to. Countless numbers have entered the 90-day residential rehabilitation program at the Bowery Mission. A concentrated ministry of counseling, medical care, nutrition therapy, Bible study and Gospel services awakens a man to spiritual renewal within himself.

These ministries are supported solely by the voluntary contributions of individuals and by legacies and bequests. Contributions are tax deductible. Checks should be made out either to CHRISTIAN HERALD CHILDREN or to THE BOWERY MISSION.

Administrative Office: 40 Overlook Drive, Chappaqua, New York 10514
Telephone: (914) 769-9000